Cries Of A Broken Man & Screams Of A Broken Woman

Compiled by:
Vanessa Canteberry

Copyright @2018 By Vanessa Canteberry

All rights reserved. No part of this publication may be reproduced, stored in a retrieval system, or transmitted in any form or by any means electronic, mechanical, photocopying, recording, or otherwise without the written permission of the authors.

Limits of Liability Disclaimer

The authors and publisher shall not be liable for your misuse of this material. The purpose of this book is to educate and empower. The authors and/or publisher do not guarantee that anyone following these techniques, suggestions, tips, ideas, and/or strategies will become successful.

The authors and/or publisher shall have neither liability nor responsibility to anyone with respect to any loss or damage caused or alleged to be caused directly or indirectly by the information contained in this book.

TABLE OF CONTENTS

Dedication i
Introduction 1
Chapter 1: Partnership 7
Chapter 2: Substance Control 15
Chapter 3: The Gift Of Growth 24
Chapter 4: Where Did We Go Wrong? 34
Chapter 5: Unequally Yoked 43
Chapter 6: You Don't Love Me Anymore? 56
Chapter 7: Exposing Truths 65
Chapter 8: Loyal & Trust 77
Chapter 9: Abandonment 87
Chapter 10: A Blended Marriage 98
Acknowledgment 108
About the Complier 115

DEDICATION

This book is dedicated to individuals who struggle with understanding the history of a person's reactions, thus finding it difficult to communicate in order to gain the clarity to make a sound decision on how to handle one another in a positive environment.

Oftentimes relationships fall apart due to our inability to express the emotional side which, unfortunately, we don't want to discuss; however, we need to in order to heal what broke us.

We hope this book will be the catalyst that will assist people to have an open and honest conversation with reality, to own their truth, to be free and live a life of abundance.

INTRODUCTION

Regardless of your gender, you should be comfortable with sharing your emotions with those whom you have built a relationship with for them to understand where your pain and/or frustration resides. Unfortunately, this is easier said than done. We continue living in bondage, feeling that there is no point appearing vulnerable with the people we surround ourselves with; those we say we love and respect.

We continue to bottle up our feelings and break down in silence to the point we vent our frustration on others who, should not be subjected to our pain or become broken with us as a result of our refusal to voice out what we continue to suppress. Too often we are told by our loved ones to just deal with our emotions as opposed to equipping ourselves with ways of handling it. We have to know that there is a better way of expressing our emotions. We can first start by forming a sentence to release our pain.

Growing up, there were times of not knowing how to speak to people without sounding angry. It showed in the body language as well as facial expressions. I bottled up years of anger from the things I saw and experienced but had no way of communicating. The silence of carrying the burden of tears, screams, and pain breaks you mentally, physically, and emotionally if you don't get a handle on it. The frequent lashing out of short temper was becoming of me, and I no longer liked what I saw.

Just dealing with it alone builds up toxic behavior in the relationship, and its unhealthy not only to you but also to those you come in contact with. This is where the breakdown gets lost in translation. Now, as adults, we have again found a way to keep things bottled up to a certain extent, yet we expect others to deal with us breaking down and shutting people out. Can we say this is so unhealthy? You are walking around, more like a ticking time bomb with poison ready to explode at any given moment, and you want those you love to deal with it and accept that this is who you are! You are more than the expression of what others label you to be. You have yet to discover the inner person you are meant to serve, the person you need to help grow as well as overcome what broke them down too.

We are often told to keep it to ourselves, but how long can you go on walking around with poison in your bloodstream? Which is now turning into an infectious disease you can no longer get rid of?

Human beings carry emotions; however, men are taught not to show their emotional side, as it's a sign of weakness. There is a desperate need to have a deeper conversation with our men because they do have feelings and should not hide them simply because they want to uphold the generational standards that qualify them as being men.

I have to admit, seeing families such as mine unravel their feelings, after having bottled them up for years, is the most heartbreaking disease of mankind. Taking a trip down memory lane to where it all began always dug holes in souls that seemed polished on the outside. Well, at least that's what it seemed. But in the reality, it's what the generation before them had taught them, and now they find themselves repeating a cycle of "how to bottle up your brokenness until it disappears." Sad to say, it will never disappear due to your inability to release the pressure before an explosion erupts.

Most relationships end because there was no chance given to build the friendship to the point of knowing the partner well enough for them to trust you and share their most intimate thoughts and/or pain points with you. We are too busy bypassing our history simply because we don't want to relive the state of mind of being vulnerable to allow someone else in. Ask yourself, would you rather be open to sharing your truth with someone you can genuinely trust, who is willing to protect your brokenness from repeating so you can heal, move forward, and break the cycle of masking the pain and never to see a repeat of it in the next generation?

Women are taught to be strong and independent, but they, too, need to be released from the world to understand their truth. Men and women are not meant to be alone, but due to the actions of breaking down and shutting others out, we push people away. Often we build a wall and not allow anybody to climb over. It gets to the point where we start becoming more frustrated, feeling as if nobody can understand where we're coming from. How can they, when we keep the wall up so high and remain independent?

At some point, a crack will form on this wall we have built, thus creating the foundation of a sinking hole owing to the lack of proper care, which is self-care, to lift the pressure off what we had been consumed in all these years.

There are women who had developed issues with men but were determined to wear the pain to control the relationship. Although they wanted the relationship, they didn't appreciate it enough to allow the man lead. Again, picking or choosing what to address in our brokenness will eventually destroy anything we come in contact with.

On the other hand, it's not unusual to see a man break down a woman simply because he had issues with women thus, he has vowed not to appreciate a woman irrespective of the love he professes. He treats her less than her worth because of the issues he carries. This diminishes the woman's strength, and she continues to stay, despite being broken down repeatedly to the point the man can walk over her with the sole of his shoes.

Women want men to open up, but from the way they protect their heart, it may take a little bit longer for a man to share the brokenness he battles on a daily basis. He could be an amazing guy whose biggest fear is failing the mother who birthed his children simply because he is fighting his own battles of the world. But once a man reaches the point he can share a piece of his heart with you, cherish it. That means he trusts you enough to allow you to walk around his heart and place your chest against his to have your hearts beat in sync. However, engaging a man in a battle of words will shut him down to the point he suffers in silence and bottles up his emotions yet again.

Men are emotional and can share their life journey sooner if only they feel the other party can be trusted. Men are delicate, even though it seems as if they are as tough as nails. They were taught to guard their heart, but sometimes the pressure can become overwhelming, and they would like to release it. As a woman, using a man's weakness to your advantage will bring out the side of him he would rather leave in his past. When a woman gets upset to the point of bringing up a man's inner thoughts in a heated agreement, this is a slap in the face of the man.

Oftentimes, when we as women, feel we are not being heard, we become very frustrated; we break down, and then we feel like our intelligence is being questioned. There will be that one person you will be able to freely open up to without judgment, but you have to be willing to be open. It took me a long time to really appreciate the possibilities of being free and open to understanding how I was able to overcome. Pulling the band-aid off an open wound remains the best decision I've ever made because I was really able to dive in before the infection spread to my children.

Someone has to be willing to remove the band-aid from their past, and these amazing authors in this book did just that. It entails being upfront with the history that had remained undisputed for years, thus finally receiving the medal of owning your truth to heal the ones to follow. To be judged in front of a jury in order to gain the victory was not the case with these authors. They received the victory and unapologetically won cases of their past because they no longer allowed it to consume them.

When God provided me with this vision to bring authors together in sharing their stories in an intimate book, I was unsure as to how it would be viewed for many reasons.

Sharing your story is a way of helping the next person who picks it up to read, as they, too, will come to the understanding that they have a story to share. It is a thing of joy to look over the journey of your life and see how far you have come, and this makes you wonder, *Who could be bold and courageous enough to be vulnerable to heal the next generation?* These authors did just that and so much more.

We hope and pray that the stories you read in this book will empower you to push past your pain and embrace what broke you so you can do the work required to heal yourself.

Cries of a Broken Man and Screams of a Broken Woman will become the conversational book that opens up the lines of communication to allow partners to know that they both said and/or felt the same thing at one point or the other.

We hope you truly enjoy the stories of these amazing authors.

PARTNERSHIP

By
James Newkirk

Well, Dorothy, the house has finally landed on you. Where do you go from here? Like in the Wizard of Oz, there are so many different ways you can describe a partnership.

Say, for instance, just like Dorothy in Oz, you landed in a pool of singles. As you begin to find your way to that partnership down your own yellow brick road, you run into several different types; you have one partnership where you know what you want, they know what they want, but they're not sure if you are right. You're not sure if they're the right fit, so you keep quiet, and you just go on this trend of dating, as they call it, not knowing that this is who you want, and you just date. I mean, you meet each other; you begin to date. You're like you like them; they like you; you go to dinner. You kiss, you hug, and then, all of a sudden, they're cheating on you, and you're cheating on them, but they don't know that you're cheating, and you don't know that they're cheating until one of them slips up that one not being you but the other one. So you get into a fight; you yell and scream; you argue; you get hurt; they get hurt, but in the back of your mind, you think, *I'm so glad that that is over with!*

Yeah, that's because you don't have the brains like the Scarecrow to realize that neither one of you wanted each other. In actuality, you were just supposed to meet up for that one night and to have a fling and to just 'do the do,' as they call it, and be done with it. But no, you tried to make what they call 'the one-nighter' into a forever, which definitely isn't going to work in some situation.

Now you are again alone, going along, minding your own business as normal, and you meet your tin man. Yeah, you remember him; he looks strong, looks brave on the outside, but he does not have the heart to love you, so, yeah, you continue to go to dinner just like you did with the Scarecrow. But this time, you have a few more emotions invested. So you go to dinner; you date; you go through the motions: "It's like I love you." You kiss; you, with each other, 'do the do' with more feelings. Next thing you know, days have gone by days into weeks, into months but those three little words have never been mentioned to the sincerity of "that's what you really mean." I mean, you can say "I love you" all the time, but until you really mean it, you just go through the motions "Sure, I can say 'I love you' to anybody," but are you in love with that person?

You know you will never be in love with that person. Yet you don't have the heart to tell them that you're not going to love them, and they don't have the heart to tell you that they don't love you. So you stay in it; one thing leads to another till you finally come to the decision of "I don't want to be with him/her," but you don't know how to tell them, and then, you know, they don't know how to tell you that they don't want to be with you without hurting each other.

But you know, what's so funny about those relationships or partnerships is that that's the same partnership that you know you go right into being the Cowardly Lion, not having the courage to get out of that relationship, so you just stay in it; you stay in it for convenience; you stay in it because they make you feel good; you stay in it because you are afraid that there's not going to be anyone else, but then you meet your Cowardly Lion, and you just break up with this one that you're with for no reason at all, and you just move on from one relationship right into the other, not giving yourself the time to breathe. So, now, what you brought from that other relationship, you're bringing into this one, and it's almost like you're picking up the pieces. You're saying, "Oh yes, I love you. Oh yes, you love me," and you're just together. Dinner, movies like the rest of them, and then, you know, eventually, you end up being partners, but under what circumstances?

You don't love this person a bit more than they love you, yet neither one of you have the courage to say that this is not what you want until you finally open up your eyes and realize that months and days and possibly even years have gone by, and you never asked that one simple phrase, "Are you in love with me?" and you come back with the response of "No, I'm not in love with you, and I will never be in love with you because of who I am and because of who you are," and you don't understand what those phrases are, so you just let it go from day to day, week to week until they finally do something that actually opens up your eyes, like they miss an occasional birthday even though they've been with you for the past five or six years, and you don't get a phone call until 3 or 4 days after your birthday, telling you "Happy birthday" with no explanation at all as to why they missed the birthday. They miss the family reunion that they have been going to for the past 5 years; no explanation. They miss the obvious Thanksgiving dinner, Christmas, New Year, Valentine's Day. They even have the nerve to miss spending their own birthday with you with no explanation that's when you have had enough until you finally have the courage to say "I got to let you go; I can't be with you because my heart can't take this.

What you're doing is not right for me and maybe right for you, but it's not right for me." So, yeah, you have to let them go until you finally meet that one. Now, you have to pay attention to all the signs of all the relationships, of all the partnerships that you had going on in your past, because partnership is kind of like business partnership. You can apply this to business; you can apply it to anything, but finding that one true partnership is like driving 6 hours to make sure that you're okay. And because you, too, have made a connection, when they get there, you don't understand why they're there, and it's because they love you just that much, and they want to be with you, and when they leave, you feel empty from being with them. Notice now the other relationships, partnerships did not make you feel empty at all, but this particular one does. You realize that you no longer want to be without that person, so you do what you've got to do if you have to; move if you want or have to. But in a true partnership, one thing you have to learn to do is, you have to give up the I's, you have to give up the you's, you have to give up the me's, and you have to replace them all with us and we.

I mean the partnerships that when you lay down at night,

they're up, taking care of what you worry about; things that you know that you need, they're up at night, taking care of it, not knowing that you need it, but they feel that you need it.

It's beyond completing each other's sentences; it's beyond completing each other's thoughts. It's like being ahead of what that person actually thinks; it's like your heart knows what their heart is saying. You can tell from their eyes; you can tell from their emotions; you can tell from the way they move, from the way they talk, the way they just look at you. You already know it's like you are them, and they are you, and you're one person. That is that perfect partnership I mean because, being in a partnership like that, it's like you're stepping right into their body, or they're stepping right into yours, and when you see one, you see the other. It's hard having a partnership like that; it's really hard having somebody like that who does not only have your back, but they also have you they have all of you.

This is the type of partnership where you can say you have met the wizard, you have met the one, you have met yourself. This person you can't out laugh, you can't outcry, you can't out smile, you can't out run because, while you're trying to outdo them, they're right there with you the whole time neck-and-neck.

But when that partnership is gone, what do you do? That's the partnership you want. That's the partnership you need. Basically, when it's gone, you now become an 'I,' you now become a 'me.' It's no longer 'we'; there's no more 'us.' Trying to find that partnership again will be the hardest thing you would ever do in your life. Hold on to that partnership; hold on to them, whether it's your friends, whether it's your lover, whether it's family friends, or whatever it is, that's the one that you want. You want somebody just like you; you deserve that because, when it's gone, it's gone, it's never coming back, and it's like the house is falling on you again, Dorothy, and you're back with the munchkins again, and you're trying to walk down that yellow brick road, but this time, you know what the Scarecrow looks like, you know what the Tin Man looks like, you know what the Cowardly Lion looks like, and you're off to find your wizard again.

About the Author

 James-Deric Newkirk, aka 'Deric,' is the founder and CEO of U'Neekly D'Zigned Jewelry. Born and raised in a little town called Atkinson, North Carolina, he has always had a flair for writing music, poetry, short stories. In school, he used to write his own comic books for class projects. He has always written poetry; eventually, he was to follow his passion for writing as well as jewelry-making. Not being able to choose between the two, he decided to do both.

Deric has always had a business mindset of crafting and writing. It wasn't until the loss of his spouse in 2017 that he realized that he has a lot of his own life stories and grief and history to share with others. He began writing passionately in journals, on napkins, scrap paper whatever he has in his hand. He kept a journal beside his bed and just wrote constantly, writing about his life, things he saw, things he heard, never planning to do anything with them until he had the opportunity. After the passing of his spouse, he decided not to let any of his writings, jewelry designs, his art of crafting to no longer go in vain.

Deciding to leave his full-time job, he sat down and began to work even harder than before. Deric stands on Faith, Hope, and Trust. This is not his destiny; it's just part of his itinerary. The world truly has a lot to offer, and he plans to see it all.

Feel free to stay connected with James-Deric Newkirk on Social Media at

www.Facebook.com/UneeklyDzigned
www.Instgram.com/UneeklyDzigned

SUBSTANCE CONTROL

By
Charon Shifflette

As I sit and Thank God I made it out alive, There were times I didn't think I would. After my separation, I started dating a childhood friend. Things were great to the point he would drive over an hour every weekend to my house and we would party all weekend. What could be better, right? (So I thought.) Loud music, drinking, and sleeping in while the kids had fun playing with all the grown-ups well the one's that would play with them and to the kids what's better than pizza every Friday? As the relationship grew, I thought, *Great! Maybe he could start doing things (boy things) with my sons since their father wasn't around.*

As time went on, one argument led to another. After not getting any financial help from my children's father, I thought to release the stress, I would sell my house and live closer to family that could help with my children then 4-year-old twins and a 6-year-old. My kids and I moved in with my mother. She kept the kids while I worked as assistant manager at a clothing store, which meant long hours. After hanging out one night, something happened between us. We arrived at my Mom's; my Mom wasn't home, he took me in the bedroom and beat me up and he said I better not tell. As the fights got worse, I had to start calling the cops. After calling a few times, an that seemed to often, an on duty officer would come to the home, the officer that I later became friends with, and 24 years later we're still friends. I knew not to call 911 too many times due to my previous abusive relationship. So, for the past 10 years, with both relationships, all I knew was, if I dare argued, I would be beaten up. He would say sorry, and it's to be water under the bridge.

Wow! Now things seemed to be going fine. One night, while out with friends, again, something went wrong, and he told the driver/friend to pull over. He then got out of the truck and told me to get out at this point, I just wanted to go home. He then proceeded to spit on me and toss his beer on me, but one of his male friends jumped out and told him to stop. At that point, they took me home. The male friend talked to him, now things were fine.

Another night came and went, and he got upset, and as we got back to my mom's, he beat me up. My grandparents lived in the same apartment complex, so my mom would be at my grandparent's a lot, which gave him plenty of time to do as he pleased.

Now, months had gone by, and things were going actually great between us. He then suggested we live together. *Sure!* I thought, as we had been dating for a while, and the children enjoyed being with him. We ended up renting an apartment about 30 minutes from my Mom's, we didn't need to buy furniture since I had it all from selling my house.

After a month or so of living together, he became very

controlling to the point that if anyone looked at me, or I looked in another direction he would think I wanted to be with that person. After getting home, he would take me in the bedroom or bathroom and accuse me of cheating and slap or hit me. I would turn the TV up and do my best to not cry loud so my children wouldn't hear, or I would call a girlfriend to take my children outside to play, and I would lock the door so they wouldn't walk in on him beating me up. After the beating, I would wash my face and go make lunch or dinner as if nothing ever happened.

One evening, he had his friends over, playing cards. I made appetizers, and in his eyes, I did something wrong. *Let me go to bed so he would get off my back*, I thought. Before going anywhere or doing anything, I would have to ask him if it was okay.

As the beatings kept taking place, I knew I couldn't go on being a prisoner, and I would have to figure something out. He wouldn't allow me to work, and that was a way to keep me locked up not in jail but my own hell. I ended up renewing my welfare case so I could start planning to get out on my own. Now I didn't have a job, car, or money. I had furniture but nowhere to put it since I didn't have money. If I had to go to the store, which was about 5 miles from the apartment, I would walk. He wouldn't always let me drive his truck, so I had to walk, which was okay, and he would time me, and if it took longer than he thought it should have been, he would beat me up because, in his mind, I was cheating. He said if I ever left, he would find me and break my child's arm and "shove it up his a**." Well, I was really afraid to move out. *God forbid I be the reason my child got hurt.* So I stayed.

After speaking with my police officer friend, he assured me that if I moved out, he would protect me. I trusted this friend, so I saved up my welfare checks and food stamps and lay low, planning to move out. When he (my ex) was at work, he always called me at 9 a.m. and 2 p.m. It was more like making sure I was still in the house. Finally, I called my mom and said I wanted to move, and not able to tell her why, she said, "OK, what's the plan?" I told her the plan was to save money and sneak out.

Every day, I made his lunch and walked him to the door, and again, he would do a 'roll call' at 9 a.m. and 2 p.m., and I better answer the phone. One day, I had decided to work out in the living room and not watch TV, which meant I missed his call. As I just finished getting dressed, unknown to me that he had left work, he came home. My hair was still wet as well as the shower. He said I missed his call and asked what I was doing. I said he must have called when I was in the shower. He said I must have had sex with someone, and that's why my hair and the shower was wet. I tried to explain that I had been working out and was sweaty, but he didn't believe me, so he beat me up. He went and picked up my underwear to smell them; then he went back to work.

A few days later, he let me use his truck to go to my mom's. I had called him to inform him that I was running late, and he said, "When you get back, I'm beating you up." At that point, I was afraid and tired of getting beaten up, so I asked my younger sister if she wanted to stay at my place. She said, "Sure." I kept her there for 4 days, not wanting to tell her he had been beating me up. After 4 days, he said, "If you don't take her home, I will beat you up with her here."

So I took my sister home, and when I arrived home, he beat me up.

I'm done with the nonsense, I thought. I told my mom I wanted to leave him, and not knowing why, she just said, "OK." Not long after, I contacted my ex and told him I needed to leave that place, so he rented an apartment in his name so we couldn't be found. Finally, the day before moving, I rented a moving truck and had it ready so we could move fast. Now, on the move-out day, I did my normal 6 a.m. routine, making his lunch and walking him to the door. I had my mom, sisters, and brothers waiting in the parking lot. After he left for work, they came in, and we started packing things and loading the moving truck. Now his morning routine was a 9 a.m. check-in call. I had everyone sit still as he talked on the phone. He just wanted to know why it took me so long to answer the phone, and why I was breathing hard, and if I just worked out. I said yes; we stayed on the phone, and it felt like forever. I didn't want to rush him off the phone. After hanging up, I now had until 2 p.m. for his next call. I withdrew my children from that school location, and we were GONE!

I contacted my neighbor; she said she kept hearing the phone ring. Sure, it was him. Then, shortly thereafter, he showed up at the house, and all she heard was him yelling, "NOOOOO! ..."

Now in the new place, which was only about 5–10 miles from him, my officer friend would come by or stay to make sure we were safe. As time went on, well, I was stuck, afraid to go out for fear of him seeing me, but I needed a job, and the kids were in school. By the Grace of God, I met a man that was a Manager at a car dealership. Well, every week or when needed, he would let me use a car off the lot to do errands and look for a job. Now, about 3 months later, we ran into each other on the street. Not much was said, but thank goodness he was dating someone.

Now that I had found a job, my ex was telling me who could and could not come in the apartment since the place was in his name, and I thought, *Here we go again!* So, again, I put a plan together, and I saved my money, and my mom was able to get me an apartment on the complex she was living. I was able to take a bus to work. Since I was still on government assistance, the State paid for me to go back to school to get my high school diploma. Everything that the State did in helping me, I used it as a stepping stone to move higher in life and never saw it as a way of life.

I finally had peace with that man, my ex, but it caused many problems with my officer friend. I couldn't let my guard down, so every time we argued, I was ready for him to hit me, but at that moment, he would always hug me and say, "I Love you, and I will never hit you." Finally, it hit me. *WOW! This is how it's supposed to be!* And from that day forward, I never allowed anyone to touch me, although it took a toll on our relationship. We stayed connected as friends, and still to this day, he's only a call away.

I stayed single for a while, then met another officer. We started dating, and after a period of time, we moved in together. I thought, *Oh great! Finally, maybe I can have a peaceful home.* Wishful thinking! He had two children, and he didn't really want mine around. After a period of time, my oldest son wanted to live with my sister and her husband, and I thought, *OK, sure!* Maybe my son wanted to have that male figure around since his father wasn't coming around on a regular basis, and I just had to make sure I bought whatever he needed. The officer and I were planning on moving not too far from where we were. As we approached the move-out day, I kept calling my sister, leaving her voicemails to call me back. I needed to make sure my son was OK (since I didn't have a cell) or if they were even out. Then I decided to stay home to make sure I got a hold of my sister. Finally, that evening, after repeatedly calling her, she answered and said I never left her the new number. I said, "What are you talking about? I'm calling you from the house phone." She said, "You never left the new number." I said, "Let me call you back." I called the house number, and it said, "The number you called had been changed to a non-published number." At that moment, I went to the living room and told him (my new officer friend) I needed the number. His reply was, "Your family needs to address me when they call my house." I said, "No. Actually, they need to ask, 'Is Charon there?' or 'Can I speak to Charon?' ..." We went into the bedroom to argue and he finally gave me the phone number!

At some point, I had to put another plan together, but this time, I was self-employed and at peace. One thing I have learned is, you cannot count on others when you cannot count on yourself. Know that you can do anything you put your mind to. Know that everything happens for a reason.

One thing I must always remember is to never give husband benefits to boyfriends, for when there is no commitment; it is always easier to walk out. A man falls for me by being strong, and when I become weak by giving/doing everything for him, I have found he will lose interest. I always put a plan together to never lose. I trust, but I never forget my lessons in life. I never give 100% of myself to show I am weak, for when I think I am weak, I have always noticed that the man starts to take advantage of my weakness, and then I remember who he fell in love with and that I am so much happier when I am true to myself of being so powerful. So, a few things: never lose self, always stay strong, and never stop growing.

About the Author

Charon Shifflette is a single mom with 3 boys a single and a twin. She originally starting running away from home when she was 15 years old. She dropped out of 10th grade, thinking she loved someone, and got married at 16 years. She had 3 children at the age of 18. Her ex-husband left when she was 25 years old and took ownership of the company they had together due to her not knowing the in-and-out of the business.

Regardless of what transpired, she gathered her thoughts and planned to rebuild herself for the sake of her children. She went back to school to get her high diploma and worked multiple jobs to provide for her children. She worked to build her cleaning business and is now a best-selling author. There is life after being in abusive relationships. She finally found her own strength within herself to not count on anyone and to make her own way. Now she is sharing her story with others to inspire them to the possibilities of gaining one's own inner strength to realizing one's worth.

Feel free to stay connected with Charon Shifflette on Social Media at

www.Facebook.com/CharonShifflette
www.Instgram.com/CShifflette

THE GIFT OF GROWTH

By
S.C. Urquhart

Over the course of our lives, we all tend to grow and develop both spiritually and emotionally at different rates based on various stimuli. Experiences in our lives affect us in different ways. These experiences continuously evolve the way in which we look at our lives and the way we view the world. This evolution of growth affects our lives and our decisions, and it also affects the people in our lives. We can either create positive effects on the people around us or negative effects based on our level of growth. Without growth, our souls will cry out, yearning for stability and peace. Growth then becomes one of the single most significant factors in our existence. When we take care to examine our growth under these conditions, we can see that it is vital we understand in which direction we are growing, and whether we need to make adjustments on our journey.

As many of us know or have learned, true growth often stems from pain and is sharpened through heartache and suffering. This is not always the case, as many people are able to make it through life without ever being tested. These individuals may have been born into affluence, or they may have been blessed with the gift of discernment early on. In that case, they lessened their chances of making bad decisions as a foundation to stimulate growth. Unfortunately, everyone is not blessed with this type of advantage. The fact of the matter is, many of us grow and mature through conflict and pain. As our cries and screams ring out, they can drown out everything and everyone. We find ourselves locked in conflict. This conflict can be within ourselves, in our hearts, or between our own ears. However, there is a great deal of growth that manifests itself through conflict with others. These examples of conflict will involve family members, co-workers, acquaintances, and our significant others. As men, we cannot allow our lack of maturity to permeate our relationships. One broken relationship, due to our selfish or thoughtless words and actions, will no doubt lead to more. We have to address these shortcomings and try to work on strengthening our relationships and our lives.

Growth, much like the idea of success, rarely flows in a straight line. To obtain success in life, one must take turns and detours off the main road. These detours are where conflict and other obstacles may take form. Through this conflict, one can learn valuable lessons that would otherwise not be attainable. We can then utilize these lessons to continue on the path of success. The same principles can be attributed to growth and development. Some of the greatest minds and successful people have had to do a great deal of growing so that they could build on their knowledge and experiences. Growth is a part of our natural lives, and unfortunately, there are many people who either ignore the signals for growth, or they outright resist the opportunities that can take them to their next level. Sadly, many people grow so little that they never reach the maximum capacity for their lives. That can lead to other issues. Men can become bitter about the regret over never having accomplished goals, for instance, and take that anger out on wives and children. Some women who never allowed themselves time and space to heal and grow from past relationships can bring that negativity into future relationships, setting the stage for more heartbreak and conflict. We must first learn to characterize growth for what it is, a vital component of our development.

This begs a question. If growth is necessary for ultimate peace and success, why would people ignore precious opportunities for growth? Even when they are shown the ways and means that would lead to their own development, why would they push back against this process? Well, oftentimes the process of growth begins where the comfort zone ends. In order to achieve maximum growth and success, one must be taken out of their comfort zone on a regular basis. If one is comfortable, chances are they are not challenging themselves to be more or to reach their next level. There are many people who are in this category, and they are perfectly fine with it.

The comfort zone is where people go to find regularity and routine, even if it involves negative stimuli. The comfort zone can be a stressful and sad place to be. However, this place is familiar and provides a safety net. How then can one break free from the traps of the comfort zone and take charge of their lives and their destinies? The answer involves setting a foundation. Through prayer and supplication, we can ask God to give us the strength to take a leading role in our lives. We ask Him to order our steps and to catch us when we may fall. Through this process, we will gain confidence in our abilities. Better still, we will gain confidence in our abilities to bounce back when failure hits or when opportunities fall flat. Many of us have issues with rejection, or we pull back and give up when things don't go our way. When our relationships go South, we can tend to numb ourselves from anything and everything. However, it is through that suffering that we grow. If things were to always go our way, we would not be exposed to the necessary stimuli we need to gain confidence in our abilities to fight through turmoil and despair, to reach the other side stronger and wiser.

I've had to deal with so many issues and fight through so many obstacles and tribulations before I allowed myself the space and opportunity to grow. The funny thing is, I was taken through more hardships *after* I was able to gain my strength and confidence. I would often ask God about that. *Why are You giving me more conflict now that I know You? I thought the hard part was over. Why am I still being tested?* The answer was not as obvious as it is now. Quite simply, God will always give you only what you are able to handle. The Bible reminds us that "No temptation has overtaken you except such as is common to man; but God *is* faithful, who will not allow you to be tempted beyond what you are able, but with the temptation will also make the way of escape, that you may be able to bear *it*" (*1 Corinthians 10: 13, New King James Version*). We can take peace in the fact that although God will indeed set roadblocks in our way and obstacles in our path, He will only burden us with what we are able to bear. In addition, He will design a path for us to always come through our hardship if we are strong enough and faithful enough to follow Him.

When I was battling my storms of addiction, incarceration, and failure, I did not know where to turn. I knew that I needed help, but the outlets that I reached out to provided no concrete plan of action. I was left to continue spiraling downward, and along the way, I did damage to myself and to others. I was engrossed in an ever-evolving conflict within myself and with my family and friends. I turned my back on some, and many turned their backs on me. My relationships failed, and my cries rang out. I was broken and bitter. My parents supported me, but I could tell that my bad decisions were weighing heavy on them. I did not concern myself with the work they did to raise me and show me the right way. I was trapped in a place of despair, and I did not know how to escape this awful wasteland.

When things started to go downhill for me, I began experimenting with drugs. Instead of seeing these drugs for what they were and realizing that it was only a temporary fix to a larger issue, I went further and began using them just to get through the day. As a result, my work suffered, and I stopped going to work and my undergraduate classes. I spent my days either lying around high and numb or with other users, or holed up in dilapidated areas where we could all go and get high and not be judged or even bothered. For a long time, this was my comfort zone. Being under the influence of whatever drug I was using became my safe spot. I started making terrible decisions, from stealing to swindling. I got kicked out of school and had no job and no money. I was arrested and given a break, and you would think that would be the wake-up call I needed. However, that just became the first arrest of more, and I started moving quickly towards a rock bottom that would change things forever. I was not growing, and I can recall being offered opportunities for help. Unfortunately, I wasted these opportunities, and I did not take them seriously. Why? I did not want to leave my comfort zone. I was not ready to do things right. I was not ready to give up my lifestyle, and there was nothing anyone could say or do that would dissuade me from doing exactly what it was I was doing. Meanwhile, things got worse.

When a moment of clarity is approaching, sometimes we can feel it coming. Some of us have gone through so much; we know that it is only by God's grace that we are still here alive and well. That is one of the initial realizations I had to understand to help spark a light in my spirit. My soul was trying to grow, and I could feel my spirit being pulled away from my lifestyle, and God chose the perfect setting to help me achieve this goal. Being incarcerated is a horrible thing. Conditions are usually deplorable, and hopelessness abounds. However, God used this environment to start working on me. I would say that He chose this environment because I had nowhere else to go. I became clean and sober for the first time in years, so I was forced to face all of the thoughts and fears I had spent so much time running away from and covering up. I could not hide anymore. The writing was on the wall. It was time for me to step up and address all of these issues that had held me back for so long. I was broken, and I had no choice but to pull it together and fix it.

God chose various people to come in and out of my life

during this time, and He set up situations and scenarios in just the right way to get my attention and keep me motivated and thirsting for more of His favor. I finally started to feel a sense of hope and encouragement through His careful kneading of my soul. Even in lockup, my spirit was getting stronger, and my determination was strengthening. I developed the ability to look inward and analyze the damage that I had been inflicting on myself and on those who were close to me. A strong guilt was rising in my spirit, and it forced me to put my life under a microscope. I had nothing but time on my hands, so I decided to use that time wisely. I began to pray, and I worked to chip away at my bad habits. I learned that it is not the acquirement of things that defines existence. Rather, it is the washing away of the unnecessary that will allow room for values, virtues, and a dedication to serving others. God was setting me up for the life that I had always wanted, and once His magnificence came to a startling revelation, I was no longer able to think along the same lines anymore. I was not permitted to view my existence the same way anymore. Quite simply, He would not allow me to.

I left that situation and never looked back. I cleaned up my life and made the decision that I would do everything in my power to show God that I understood what He had been trying to tell me, and I would spend my life in the service of others. My hope was that I would be able to help others who were heading down a similar path to mine. I wanted to warn them and help them refocus. This is still my goal today, and this will be my goal forever. After so much pain and conflict, I was finally able to grow. Growth was a foreign concept for me because I could not accept it. It had to happen in God's time. Now that I am aware of the powerful nature of growth, I welcome challenges and opportunities to learn through peril and expand my strength. As a result, my relationships have been restored and strengthened, and as a man, I can truly love my wife and family from a place of strength and not uncertainty. Through God's grace, I fixed my brokenness, and anyone can achieve the same success.

This is what we must strive to understand and live by. If you are struggling with life and the direction your life is heading, there is hope. There is always hope. The key is that you must be ready to accept this help and this hope; otherwise, you will spin wheels and waste time until God sees fit to save you from yourself. Many people will never pick up on the signs that God will place before us. It took me quite some time to understand what it was He was attempting to show me. Even when I realized what was happening, I still looked away. I wanted to remain in my comfort zone. However, I have learned about the perils of the comfort zone. It is sometimes a dangerous place to be, and if we are not careful, a deadly place indeed.

Growth, then, is essential to developing ourselves and developing our relationships with others. We cannot expect healthy relationships with others until we have a healthy relationship with ourselves. We cannot expect healthy relationships with ourselves until we have first developed a healthy relationship with God. He will guide us in the direction we must go so that we will no longer view our issues as obstacles placed to deter and destroy us. We will understand that these obstacles are for our good, and through our power and resilience, we will stimulate growth and take the next step in our development. Afterward, we will have the capacity to obtain, maintain, and sustain our lives. We will serve as a beacon of hope to others who are struggling to stimulate their own growth. We can show them the way and do our part in helping someone else escape their brokenness and embrace their growth.

About the Author

S.C. Urquhart is an author, scholar and life coach. He is a Virginia native, and he has served in the education field for almost a decade. S.C. obtained his Bachelor of Arts degree in English studies from Virginia State University. He holds a Master's degree in Education, Curriculum and Instruction from Averett University and an Educational Specialist degree in Education Leadership from Liberty University. S.C. is currently pursuing his Doctoral degree in Education Leadership at Liberty University.

He works as a Program Director for a workforce development initiative, helping students master various disciplines as they work toward their high school diplomas, industry-recognized certifications, and GEDs. S.C. mentors to young people and enjoys opportunities to share his story of tragedy and triumph. S.C. enjoys spending time with his wife and children, and he holds a special love for music, history, writing, and astronomy.

Feel free to stay connected with S.C. Urquhart on Social Media at:

www.facebook.com/scinspires
www.instagram.com/scinspires
www.twitter.com/scinspires
www.scinspires.com

WHERE DID WE GO WRONG?

By
Dr. Aikyna Finch

When I look back at the relationships in my life, I know I am the common factor in all of them, as most of them went on to get married after dating me. I also know that I don't settle well, and I make it difficult for the people that make me feel that I am in that position. I have standards in my life, but I also want love, so it is hard to decide which way to go in that situation. As a career woman, I wanted to see and fulfill my fullest potential. I knew there was a chance that love would not be included on my journey of ultimate success, but I had to go on the journey anyway. Along the way, I kissed many frogs, but none of them turned into my prince. I'm still on this journey alone, and as I get older, I'm still not really okay with that. At the end of the day, I have to realize that my heart was meant to love someone and to be loved in return. So, what do you do when the only thing in life that you want is something you can't have? I guess in this instance you have to ask the question, where did we go wrong?

The men in my life have been interesting, to say the least. Out of all the men in my life, I would say I could've had a future with three of them. Each of them had their own flare and uniqueness that attracted me to them. They also had their own way of giving me what I wanted, which was to be needed. In my youth, I didn't get a lot of male attention because I was considered a nerd. I wasn't in the popular group, so I didn't get to experience a lot of the boyfriend-girlfriend interactions until I was 16. That is where I met Man 1. He was 6 months younger than me and probably the longest male figure in my life. We had an on again, off again deal for about 10 years. I was mean to him, and the meaner I was, the more attracted he was to me. I did have feelings for him; I just felt that he was too nice. I felt he was too soft and that he would just give me my way all the time and not tell me when enough was enough or when I stepped over the line. In actuality, he was letting me be me. He knew that I was a pistol and a spitfire and that to cage me was the wrong thing to do. Instead, he just loved me for who I was, but I was too young to see that at that time—what acceptance really was. I would love to have that today in my life. My family adored him and still do to this day. He ended up getting married and had three kids. I don't think that we would have ended that way if we got married, but if we did, then I probably wouldn't have been the person that I am today. I sometimes think of him and realize that I did miss out on a good person. I probably owe him endless apologies, and it still wouldn't be enough. At the end of the day, he ended up with what I wanted in life, so he ended up being the lucky one out of the two of us.

Man 2 happened when I was finishing my doctorate

degree. He came to my office for service in February and, in the process, flirted with me. I kept it strictly professional, and I didn't see him again until June that same year. I was working on a computer, and this man walked in and said something to me as I was working. I turned around to say something rude because I thought it was another Soldier, and instead, it was this gentleman standing there, smiling at me. He was so sweet and nice and was all about me. Eventually, we started dating. After we started dating, I found out that he had a baby on the way in about 4 months. As you can tell, this relationship started off crazy, and it would end crazy. We broke up in September, yet we were together every day for the next year-and-a-half. Even though we never said we were boyfriend and girlfriend again, we lived as if we were. It was an interesting situation because he ended up having PTSD and a little baby, so I was appointed his caregiver. This man was not educated, but he taught me so much. He taught me about unconditional love and seeing people for who they are. He taught me how to be free and to let my guard down. He taught me how to be open to different experiences and to love even when you've been hurt. He showed me what a good heart looked like and how love should feel like. This was my first interaction with falling in love with a man and with his child. This baby showed me that I could actually be good with children, and I had skills. Before then, I didn't think I was ever going to have children or even be good at it because I was so career-driven, but this little baby changed my whole perspective on the idea of having a family. When I lost the man, I lost the baby too. I had to admit to myself that I missed them both. I missed the idea of having two people waiting on me when I get home from work, wanting to spend time with me and making me feel needed. The aftermath of that situation stunned me for a while. I came out of it a little wounded and a lot hurt in my spirit. He ended up marrying the baby's mother and had another son. After 3 years of marriage, she left him high and dry. He called me, and then I got to say "I told you so." I got to say all the things that I wanted to say because I was hurt, and he just listened and apologized for hurting me. He wanted to try again, but I remembered how much energy and time it took to be with him, and I had to decline the offer. Would he have loved me? Yes, and I know he would have, but I'm on a self-discovery journey right now, and I have to see it through. Being with him would have taken me off that journey completely and turned all my focus on him. So, why does a person who wants love turn it down? Because not all love is good love. Love should enhance you, not hinder you. I shouldn't have to bury my dreams just to know love.

Man 3 happened when I was in my higher educational career, and I was flying high. I was making a name for myself, and I was climbing the ranks, and I was feeling good. This person was degreed, tall, handsome and slick. He knew how to push my buttons and wasted a lot of my time and energy over a 5-year time span. He caused many fights between me and my family. He was the master manipulator. So how did I fall for this one? He had health problems, and he was misunderstood, but so was I, so I related with him. We talked on the phone a lot, and one day, he said, "There is a reason why I call you every day," and that was the beginning of an interesting phase in my life. This person was hurt and broken and intended on never feeling or being hurt again. So I went on a mighty roller coaster ride of emotions because of it. It is the weirdest thing when your mind says no, and your heart says yes. It changes a lot of your thoughts and decisions in ways that you sometimes can't recognize. I loved him on a level that I had never loved another man. I did things just to make him happy and to make him smile, yet, in the two years that we were supposedly together, I never was invited to his home or met his children. He wanted me to help him, so when I was in higher education administration, it was all good, but when I started on the path to social media and speaking, he said our career paths were too different. There were so many signs that he was wrong, but on paper, he was perfect, and I needed this to work. We broke up for two years; then he came back, and we tried again, but that didn't work either. I got to say everything I felt about him and how I was treated, but in the end, I left that situation broken, and I am still healing from it to this day. I tried to love one more time, and they were just looking for a sugar mama, so that ended, but from Man 3, I learned not to let things linger when it is not working. People do not have time for that when they can be working on their next level.

In the end, I realize that it was not all them, and it was not all me, but I am the common denominator. I wanted to be loved so bad that I tried to make crazy situations work because they made me feel needed, and that was what I just really wanted in life. As I get older, I realize that I was not meant to settle, and these men were not meant for me. In the grand scheme of things, they were meant to teach me a lesson. They were in my life for a reason and a season, and I tried to turn them into a lifetime. God has a way of giving you lessons that you need to know without letting you know you need to know them. Each one of these men taught me something about myself that I wouldn't have known if I didn't have the experience. They taught me that I'm stronger than I thought, smarter than I thought, tougher than I thought, and more worthy than I thought. It makes a lot of sense that you would just go after your dreams, but you can't make anyone love you, and you can't change anybody's mind. It may not be in the cards that I find love in this life, but it's not in the cards that I settle either. Life is very interesting. It will take you on journeys that you need to go on, it will take you on journeys that you don't want to go on, and it won't let you know the difference. All you know is that you're riding the ride for whatever it's worth. From the rides with these three men, I realize that the blessing is in the lesson. The lesson of how to listen, how to feel, how to know, and how to love. Many people don't get this lesson in life; I'm thankful that I received the lesson.

Even though my journey with these three men is complete, my journey for love is not. From these three men, I have learned that I'm not the only deciding factor in things, that I need to listen to the other person the way that I want them to listen to me, and I need to let all of my barriers and guards down in order to be loved not in the perfect way, but the right way. So, when I ask myself the question, "Where did we go wrong?" I will say the answer is miscommunication, selfishness, disrespect, and misunderstanding. This is on both sides, but mostly on my side. I had to realize that the world didn't revolve around me, no one was going to stop their world for me, and I wasn't going to be the most important person in anybody's life. I made men feel like they weren't good enough, and the way that they loved me wasn't good enough. That was not fair because they were good enough, and the way they loved me was good enough. I was just stuck in a fantasy that happened for other people but was not meant to happen for me. I let love pass me by because it didn't look the way I thought it should look. If I were to let go and just let life happen, there is no telling where I would be in love. I have learned that love can't be controlled. You can't make people love you, and not everyone is built to be in a relationship. I know I am built to be in a relationship, but I know that it can't be with just anyone. They are going to be an enhancer, a rock, a leader, and a teacher. At the end of the day, I rather ask, "Where did we go wrong?" than "Where did my life go?"

About the Author

Dr. Aikyna Finch is a Podcaster, Social Media Coach and Speaker. She is also a Forbes Coaches Council Member. She coaches in the areas of Empowerment, Life, and Social Media at the individual and groups levels from her company Finch and Associates LLC. She co-hosts the Motivate Social Podcast by her company Changing Minds Online. She speaks about Motivation, Education, and Social Media and avidly live streams on these topics.

Dr. Aikyna Finch is an Educator and Author. She received a Doctorate in Management, MBA in Technology Management and Executive MBA from Colorado Technical University. She has a Masters of Management in Marketing Management from Strayer University and Bachelors in Aeronautical Technology in Industrial Electronics from the School of Engineering of Tennessee State University. Her teaching disciplines include business, leadership, marketing, social media, and information systems at the graduate and undergraduate levels.

She is the Co-Author of six books and launched her first solo project, <u>Motivation Ignited</u>, in November of 2016. She is a Contributor to the Huffington Post, Goalcast, Forbes, Shine Now Magazine. She has been interviewed and featured on Huffington Post, Hello Beautiful, Women

Speakers Association, and many others. Dr. Aikyna Finch has spoken on many platforms, including the Periscope Summit, Women In Leadership Summit, The Boldly Empowering Entrepreneurs Conference, The Business Vlog Summit, and many more!

Feel free to stay connected with Dr. Aikyna Finch on Social Media at

www.Facebook.com/DrADFinch
www.Instgram.com/DrADFinch
www.Twitter.com/DrADFinch
www.Linkedin.com/in/DrADFinch
www.aikynafinch.com

UNEQUALLY YOKED

By
Sheena Moton

"A couple can identify with being yoked together as being united to each other for a common goal or purpose."

In the Bible, Paul said we are not to be united to someone who does not pursue the pursuits we have as a Christ-follower. We must not and should not join others when they pursue something that is not of God.

REFLECTIONS

Over 20 years ago, there was a young girl who thought she knew exactly what she wanted in life. She had visions of owning a home, an education as a physician, married with 3 children, a fancy car, traveling around the world and the whole nine yards. This young girl loved to journal and draw out her life as it looked to her. She had quite the imagination, always daydreaming about a 'perfect world.' Constantly pulling into her imagination because, in reality, she was far from perfect. She never wanted anyone to know that she was suffering from loneliness and a burning desire to be loved.

It really didn't matter how she got the love; all that mattered is that she was the center of LOVE. She had no idea of what Real Love looked or felt like. But that was fine with her because she had the boyfriend of her dreams. Both of them were well liked in their neighborhoods, high school, and even the church community. She was quite the singer and enjoyed dancing-ballet, tap, and jazz, while he was an all-star athlete, varsity football player and enjoyed being a ladies' man.

Her man is kind, loving, thoughtful, athletic, good looking and can cook! She was quite certain that one day, they would make the marriage of the century and knew instantly that if he asked her to marry him, their wedding would be to die for. She can only imagine how her life would be as a married woman. She is so excited that someone loves her enough to consider her to be their wife. I bet that everyone will anticipate this wedding day, except for a few, but they will get over it. On a Sunday afternoon, she sketched the layout for their wedding day for the 100th time. It was sunny outside, but somehow, there was a gentle cool breeze that brushed against her cheek. She sat on her grandmother's deck, drinking lemonade and listening to her favorite 90's jams.

Unconditionally, he loves her! It really doesn't matter if her mother doesn't like him. He's not her boyfriend; he's all hers. Well, at least he is now at this moment; these females out here have nothing else to do but to keep calling on his phone. She is a no-nonsense kind of girl. Not having time for this mess. He is hers, and she is his, she said often. Nothing will come between them. She is tired of hearing that they have no idea what it takes to be married or that love means more than just saying "I love you." Everyone wants to be an expert on marriage nowadays. Their love will last forever—she's sure of that.

It really does not matter the age; she is growing up, and her high school sweetheart will be her husband. She will get married because love has found her. He that findeth a good wife, findeth a good thing, right? She is going to get married. She will be the only one that matters once he marries her. Don't they know that marriage is the glue that keeps the relationship together? We are evenly yoked. She grew up in a Baptist Church, and he did too, so she is certain that with God before them, they will never separate. *My fiancé does know of God!* Once they are married, they will go to church as a family. A lot of things will change. I hear wives help to make changes for their husbands, and they give them this list—the 'honey do this or that' list. Yeah, that's it!

His family loves me, including his mom. It took a while for his grandmother to warm up to me after that time I came to her house in those bootie shorts and tank top. That's all a thing of the past now. Even though he swears he is not a momma's boy, I beg to differ sometimes. It does drive me nuts because he wants me to spend a lot of time with his momma. He will disappear for hours and have me just chilling with his mother until he decides to show up. Is she supposed to be my babysitter? Maybe he does it because he loves us both so much and hopes that we will become like mother and daughter. Yes, that is it. But in the Bible, I hope he knows that it says cleave to your wife.

"Therefore shall a man leave his father and his mother,

and shall cleave unto his wife: and they shall be one flesh" (*Genesis 2:24, KJV*). I hope he realizes that cleaving is key in building a marriage that will endure hard times and be the beautiful relationship that God intends it to be.

SEARCHING

I've been searching for so long to fill the empty void that was within me. It was quite challenging for me being a teenage mom at age 16. And when I got pregnant again at age 18, I had no choice other than to keep myself together. No one would ever know how I was really feeling. I was yearning to have a family and was determined to be married too. Spending time trying to fill a void, rushing to paint a picture that made everything in my world look great was now my specialty.

We were similar, yet different. We talked about finances, raising our children, household chores, dreams, visions, and so much more. Daily, it seemed like our thoughts were becoming one. I can't wait to be committed to being his bride. He gave me a sense of security. This is almost too good to be true. And then, it happened; he asked me to marry him, and of course, I said Yes! The ultimate vision a wedding day is going to happen. My fiancé let me take the lead. His answer was always "Whatever you want." Wow, this is going to be easy. Men aren't supposed to be interested in wedding planning anyway.

I was sadly awakened from that dream too. My fiancé walked into our living room and said, "We are spending way too much money on your ideas of a dream wedding.

Your dream is not my dream. It is not reality, and you need to stop it. We cannot afford all of that. We can just show up in timberlands and a sweatsuit. Yes, that will be just fine." I looked at him as if to say "You have to be joking." His look toward me showed me that his statement was no joke! What was I to do now? Who is going to show up to a wedding with that crazy attire? So, back to my grandmother's deck I go. I drew up another plan for our wedding. This time, it included no one but he and I as well as the Officiant. This will make him happy.

Yes, we will get married in timbs and a sweat suit, but no one else will have to know. I love him, and he loves me. This is a minor disagreement. The bride and groom usually have differences before they get married.

It's August 12th, and we traveled to get our marriage license, and even though we did not have timberlands and sweat suits on in the heat of Summer, we did wear 4th of July shirts from Old Navy and blue jeans. What kind of foolishness is this? Why am I letting him win? Because it's part of being a good wife to be. Being submissive that's all I need to do.

We are married now. It's only been a couple of hours, and we are already having inconsistencies on how we are going to save money. Even though we did not have a big wedding as planned, we spent money like it was crazy because we had people that had invested in our wedding and wanted their money back. He was paying people out of my bank account, and I was paying people out of his. Who was really keeping track?

We have these two young boys, and we are looking at each

other sideways because he wants to discipline them his way (the dad's way), and I want to just talk to them (the nurturer's way). Our parenting skills are changing because we are married now. Or at least that's what I think. Everyone appears to be happy for the two of us, but I can't help but feel like something in our relationship isn't right. I am just ready to get to the happy times that they talk about in the movies. There happy times in a marriage, right? Somebody help me, please! There has to be more to this marriage stuff. Who signed up for disagreements, arguing, and fussing, Not I? I will remind him in the morning that I married him so that I could have a perfect life. I shall have the life that I envisioned.

DAYDREAMING

"Marital intimacy—the act of love that is never to involve anyone else"

As the pitcher fell to the floor, she realized that she had been day-dreaming yet again on what her life was supposed to look like. What happens after marriage? Everything appeared to be in perfect shape until she ended up pregnant with their 3rd child. Who does that? Who goes out and gets pregnant before they have purchased their house, fancy car, and even became a doctor? All she wanted was love. She had seen her mother and father unite in marriage for over 20 years. That failed as she became an adult, resulting in a divorce that was long overdue. They worked hard 'separately' to give their daughter what they thought she deserved when all their daughter wanted was to be loved unconditionally by her parents and to be in a home with the both of them. It seems like history is repeating itself. Her husband wants to be a strong provider of his now family of 4.

Being a good wife and dealing with heavy levels of testosterone is challenging for her. Because of her past issues of feelings of loneliness and loveless, she was no longer able to see happiness because she was not at the place that she had dreamed of over and over again. The young couple who are trying to adjust to marriage and children now seem to be unequally yoked! Thoughts of emotional distress plague both of them. She didn't see it, and he didn't ask about it. It's starting to become apparent that they are not happily married at all. Their parents noticed, the children saw it first-hand, and God is sending messages that He is aware too.

The 'leave and cleave' in the marriage bond is also a picture of the union God wants us to have with Him. 'Ye shall walk after the LORD your God, and fear him, and keep his commandments, and obey his voice, and ye shall serve him, and cleave unto him' (*Deuteronomy 13:4, KJV*).

THE IMPACT: Marriage

The days are running together. You don't notice me, and I must be invisible to you. Why are we putting so much energy and time into being the busiest people? Do you even know that I want you to notice me? I no longer have the energy to care about what you need. You don't care about me. You haven't acted interested in my desires for a very long time. Two can play that game; I won't be interested in what you want to do either. Let's see who holds out the longest. The test will tell who will be the strongest. Now let's wait and see. NO arousal, sex, love, comfort, compassion, or partnership communication. You don't understand me. Can't you see how mad and disappointed I am with you? All the while, you feel like I have left you on the side of the road with two flat tires. You have an inside tug that says it wants to share your heart with me. But there is no way that could ever be possible. I can not even begin to understand what this is, I only know that we are on the wrong page.

We need to talk, but talking may be too risky for us. It's not like you understand me anyway; you are clearly not liking me. Yes, I said it. You can love me all you want, but do you like me? There is a difference. I used to feel safe in your arms, but I wonder what it would look like to be comforted by another. Oh, no, that sounds crazy. Is that what he wants me to do, turn to someone else? I shall not, for no matter how my flesh calls out, he should know that he is the only extinguisher.

Why does it seem like I am getting closer to God, and He is growing further from him and me at the same time? I have made so many mistakes and I know that I am not perfect, but who is?

Who is the head of the household? Women are not designed to be the head. The man is the head, and the woman is the helpmate. This is by design and should not be a choice. I didn't realize how much of a control freak I really was until I asked my husband to make some sacrifices for me. I made up some random demands, and he chose not to do them. I never knew how fast I could get into my feelings by hearing my spouse tell me the word NO. I never thought I was asking for too much. I wanted him to be the PERFECT man that was in my dreams. I want all the bills paid; I want him to have the perfect job, always take care of me and do some domesticated stuff too. I just want to go to work. I don't want to have to cook, clean, do homework with the kids. I just want to be a 'Well Kept' woman with limited responsibilities. Wait, that doesn't even sound right. I feel as though my husband did not give me enough fight, and I was allowed to control a situation that he was to take the lead on. Why do women do that? Why do we feel like it's OK to step into a man's place that was not meant for us to be in? Just because we are in a new age where women are more independent does not mean we have authority to try and replace what God designed, which was for the husband to be the head of this home. Because I wanted control, our families' path took a different turn. Instead of the being equal, we were becoming more divided. I never knew that this could happen when you put yourself in a situation instead of taking it to God.

"God takes His design for marriage seriously. Leaving and cleaving is God's plan for those who marry. When we follow God's plan, we are never disappointed."

MY HEART SAYS NO MORE

I feel so disconnected from him. I want to be one with him. I need him, but I feel so separated. For the past years, we have cried separately, yelled at each other, said things to hurt each other's feelings and devalued our gifts. I want to be close to you, but I'm too stubborn to let you into my space. I know you want me to be closer to you, but you won't give me the opportunity to know that you are that vulnerable as a man, yet I see you cry when you think I am not near. Silent tears because of his past hurts, cherished memories of his grandmother (may she rest in peace), inabilities of goals not reached. But if we don't communicate, the tears remain silent. He thinks I do not care.

Hurt people, hurt people that's an old phrase. It's hard for me to share what's in my heart with him. I enjoy mostly sharing the ugliest sides of me with him instead. Reaching into that ugly part of me gives me great pleasure. I enjoy cussing him out behind his back, nagging him to death, expressing anger, despair, and frustration too. It always will be his fault. He's been the blame for a long time. No one told him to love me; he does love me. Continuing down this road will leave us stuck. We are both contributing to each other's bad love habits.

On the outside, we are trying to be the perfect married couple like we started out to be in my dreams. Those days are long gone; I wonder if we'll ever get back to the way we were. Tired of the pain, the sense of being alone, the unfulfillment. Is this how love is supposed to feel like? Now we are throwing shade at each other's friends. I see them as the enemy too.

Spreading lies and deceit has become a game for the both of us. Why do we even listen so much to those friends? They are not even married. They have no idea of what it takes to make a marriage work but are quick to give information as if they are the 'Expert.' They don't realize that the differences that I and my spouse have may actually lead us back to the light. I pray that we are able to pray like before, talk like before, love like before. I'm am so lost in the silence and depression that plagues now that we are in a divided space.

ADVICE

Take your time when thinking about marriage. Revert back to what the Bible says as it relates to unequally yoked. What does your heart say? What are your desires? There is nothing on earth that will keep your spouse with you in a happy marriage if you can't agree on anything. Be honest and true to yourself. There are many levels of disagreement, and we have learned that because we choose to disagree. It does not make us unequally yoked; it simply just means we were not called to do the same thing.

I and my husband just needed to be reminded that it's important to communicate openly. It's OK to agree to disagree as long as we consider each other's points of view. It wasn't until I needed him and because I was hurting he realized how much I had always longed for him to take the control that I stole from him. I know now that he just needed me to be his wife, love and cherish him and to be the helpmate; his companion, supporter. Yes, God chose me be my husband's helper!

About the Author

Sheena Moton is The Empowerment Planner of Eventz N Thingz Planning Services. She creates events that Empower, Inspire and bring about Change in Women who are seeking to go to their next level personally and professionally.

She is also an author, speaker and mentor who her mentees have coined as **#TheChangeAgent** helping them to remove **"Unhealthy Beliefs"** that have plagued their careers, mindsets, and goals. Sheena encourages the women to level up through those past experiences and Release their Inner SuperHero. She also hosts an annual women's empowerment conference titled "Women with Big Hats." She sits on the Board of Directors as Secretary for Love by the Handles, a Non-Profit agency helping to serve Women and their children who have been affected by the acts of Domestic Violence.

She resides in the DC Metropolitan area with her amazing husband and 5 loving sons. Her first experience as a published author was in September 2017 for the book Breaking Free Forever-*The Momentous Journey*, which was a book compilation with three amazing co-authors. She embraced the spirit of writing and is now overfilled with joy, as she is a part of this anthology titled *Cries of a Broken*

Man and Screams of a Broken Woman! You will be able to feel the experience as she shares her chapter of **"Unequally Yoked!"**

Feel free to stay connected with Sheena Moton on Social Media at

www.Facebook.com/SheenaMotonInspires
www.Instgram.com/SheenaMotonInspires
www.sheenamotoninspires.com

YOU DON'T LOVE ME ANYMORE

By
Dr. Elaine Dilbeck

As I began to write this chapter, I was unsure of where to begin. I just recently experienced one of the most traumatic events in my life. After 13 years of being together, my significant other decided he did not want me to be a part of his life anymore. The reason may shock some of you, and others may say, "Who cares?" This reason, which lasted over the period of the 13 years to its final straw in October, almost took my mind and sanity. The pressure began and escalated to the point that I even contemplated taking my life. "Why so serious?" you may ask. I was so in love and attached to this man that I could not see my life without him.

He would do such things as taking me to a gay campground one year where clothing was optional. He would ask me to look at the men and pick one and tell him how I liked their manhood, and who had the largest. He wanted me to take my clothes off, telling me that I didn't need to worry, the men were gay. He just wanted me to be more comfortable being naked with other men. I can remember just praying that God would take me or get me out of that situation. He could not become excited or complete an orgasm without me talking about what he wanted to hear or him eventually demanding me to be with other men. When you are a therapist, it is difficult to take the advice you would give a client when it comes to your own situation. I am a trauma specialist and help people through their trauma every day. I encourage those who have suffered at the hand of others that I will help them through their nightmares but still could not understand why he was acting the way he was acting.

He dictated the things he wanted me to say and what he wanted to see and how it should be done to please him. He wanted me to pick the men, and he would provide the hotel room and whatever I wanted or needed. He would watch porn movies or watch the interactive live cams to feel more justified in what he was asking me to do. He would tell me that I treated him like a criminal for asking for what he wanted. Watching other couples, he felt that there was nothing wrong with it. He became defensive and angry at me. When I refused, he asked me to leave. A few weeks went by, and he asked me to come and get my stuff. He would text me and tell me, "Just make me a movie, and you can come home."

I felt as though I should do anything I could to keep him, including going against my beliefs, my values, and all reasoning. He gave me no reason to want to hang onto him, telling me that he had only asked me to marry him because he didn't want to lose me; he never had any intention on marrying me. Later, he would tell me that he wished he didn't love me and I didn't love him. But I still felt that I needed to do whatever he wanted to keep this man who didn't want to marry me and wished he didn't love me. I tried to do what he wanted and felt he needed me to do. He said if I could just talk to him in bed and make up the stories he needed, all would be fine. I did, and eventually, that did not work. I even went as far as to discuss it with a male friend if he would help me to do what this person wanted me to do. I tried to control the situation, but it got out of control. What tore this relationship apart after all this time? What was the final straw? He wanted me to have sex with other men while he watched.

He had been horribly, sexually abused by mostly males in his family while he was growing up. To calm some of the triggers and pain in his mind, he became obsessed with sex. He questioned his sexuality at times but could not act on it. He used his past marriages and relationships to satisfy this discord in his life. He would be unfaithful in his relationships, being with other women to prove he did truly love being with women. I know at some point he did truly love me, but this torment became more than he could bear.

Desperate to return to my home, I would take pictures from porn sites that did not show any faces and send them to him, telling him they were me. He was happy and would ask me questions, telling me that he was excited and could now 'get off,' but soon, even that did not please him. He wanted that movie. Baiting me with promises that I could come home. All lies! The lies became so bad that he would text me, threatening me, accusing me of things I didn't do—such as calling people and telling them what was going on. He wanted to let the outside world believe that we were still together, while he attempted to control me and the situation. So, let me now tell you why he wanted what he wanted.

Male to male sexual abuse will sometimes cause the male victim to question their sexuality, and they may experiment with the confusion they attempt to understand or find the answer to the confusion. They may also become very sexual, using female partners to have sex with other men so they can live fantasies with the men through the female. They will sometimes become what I have learned to be 'cuckolds,' which means 'the husband of an adulteress,' which is a fetish; it is meant to be an insult. It is a kind of humiliation, which can come in many forms. They have fantasies; they have a woman that other men desire; they want to explore male sexuality, which starts before they use the woman to fulfill the fantasy of being with the man. This fetish is almost always the man's and not the woman's. He may be trying to compete with the other men in what is called 'sperm wars.' The woman usually becomes burned out becoming resentful and feeling controlled by the man.

The man usually does not want it to stop. They may become addicted to porn with male on male or male on female watching the female in porn have sex with other men while her boyfriend or spouse watches. He encouraged me to watch these videos, saying, "Just find one that you can get into and enjoy." He was obsessed with the size of other men's genitals and the amount of 'cum,' along with the color of it as well. He would have me describe the taste of any man that I had had oral sex with in the past. I even made up stories of men in the past that I had not been with. I have never had to fight so hard with a man to be faithful to him. When I asked him if he would ever worry if I developed feelings for another man doing this, he would answer, "Probably, but not likely, because you know what you have here, and you're not willing to lose it. I am willing to wait on you hand and foot. You don't have to worry about anything. You just can't become emotionally involved with them. It's just sex and know you're pleasing me."

It is sad to know that all of this can come from the sexual abuse in families. I have experienced some of the things mentioned above or know someone who has. The persons I know are not in my family; the abuse occurred in their family. It appears that sexual abuse has increased over the last few years. The fact is that people are coming forward more than they would have years ago. Even though the abuse is reported more, the cases have not decreased. We now have the ability through such avenues to record and report abuse. But again, this has not detoured families from this kind of abuse of one another. The sad reality is that victims will rarely turn their family member in; therefore, very rarely are they prosecuted. It is more likely that a stranger would be caught and turned in than those who offend in a family.

When I finally cleared out most of my things, making some sort of peace with the fact that he was just going to lie to me and lead me on, I knew at some point that I could never go back even if he found the error of his ways and said: "Come home." I could never allow myself to go back into that chaos and drama. It almost cost me my sanity and my life. I feel that I have become more aware of the way I see men, and those things that I chose to ignore could no longer be ignored. By the way, I am a recovering co-dependent.

My addiction was bad and unhealthy relationships. Unhealthy men could sense this in me; these were the men that I was attracting. Until I sought out the kind of help that I needed to understand where this co-dependent behavior came from, I would never understand what a good, healthy relationship would look like. I still have triggers regarding him; it was not always bad. But now I realize what a blessing he gave me. If he had not done what he did, I would not have what I have now. I beat myself up less now. How stupid I was for allowing him to control me like that! My colleagues told me repeatedly that I was too educated for this; I deserved better than to be treated this way.

How could I be so upset over a man that did not care about me to put me through his darkness and sickness? I do realize that I deserve better than this. I deserve a man that loves me for who I am and will treat me with respect. I am not so ready to jump out there with just anybody. I am now choosy who I want to talk to and to be around. I put them through a questioning process, not an interrogation, but I know the right questions to ask now. I don't seek after just anyone's attention anymore to be treated with respect. I understand now that I have a purpose in the world, and that is, help those who have lost their way to help them, to restore back to them their sense of purpose, sense of self, sense of worthiness, their life. I thought I was helping others until I went through this life-changing event. Now I can truly say to them, "God can truly heal and restore; I know because I was once lost in the chaos, not being able to see the light. I once was lost, but now I see."

About the Author

Dr. Elaine Dilbeck was born in a small town in Tennessee and has moved many times over her lifetime. She is a sexual abuse survivor, formerly battered woman, recovering co-dependent. Both sides of her family carry the generational curse of sexual abuse and substance abuse. There came a time that she felt this curse needed to end.

She is using her and her families' stories to help others, to know they are not alone. She has experienced unhealthy relationships and understands the struggle to find oneself. She started out wanting to teach other professionals to want to help families as well. IT IS TIME for the TRAUMA to stop in families.

She received her BA in Psychology, MA and EdD in Counseling Psychology, completing a post-doctoral certificate in Clinical Foundations of Trauma. She is a Licensed Professional Counselor with the state of GA and a certified Clinical Supervisor with the LPCA. She is certified as a Trauma Service Specialist and is also a Certified Family Trauma Professional. Dr. Elaine has worked in the mental health field for more than 10 years. She currently has over 100 hours of training in trauma and PTSD, including training with Star providers who train civilian providers to work with active and former active duty military. A presenter at several conferences on trauma/PTSD, Dr. Elaine holds trainings and workshops on PTSD/ trauma, teaching other mental health professionals how to recognize and treat trauma. She is a member of Chi Sigma Iota counseling honor society. She has 5+ years' experience working with corrections as a mental health counselor as well as working with addictions.

Feel free to stay connected with Dr. Elaine Dilbeck on Social Media at

www.Facebook.com/elainedilbeck
www.Instgram.com/drd_ptsd
www.Linkedin.com/in/drelainedilbeck
www.renewurmind.com

EXPOSING TRUTHS

By
Divine Warren

Sitting here thinking about this wonderful opportunity that was presented to me. I'm wondering if this can be a blessing in disguise. Could me sharing aspects of my life really help someone? Thoughts upon thoughts began to unravel in my mind. They were coming fast, one after another. I narrowed them down to some of the ones I feel impacted me the most during times in my life.

My name is Divine. I grew up in the projects in Brooklyn, New York the Brownsville section to be exact. I remember it being a good place to live in my eyes as a child. I had a lot of friends. We had a lot of fun playing together. I think most of us were kind of naïve to the things that were going on around us. There were a lot of things going on in apartments throughout the projects that weren't spoken about. For most of my childhood life I lived with my mom, grandmother, grandfather, and little brother. My little sister came along later down the line. I can't really complain about my upbringing. My mom did everything she could to provide for us. I remember her working nights and going to college in the daytime. I also remember her being tired a lot but she continued to do what she had to do to put food on the table. Having my grandmother and grandfather around made it so much better. I always felt loved and taken care of. My grandmother was the person who mostly stayed at home. She would cook, clean, and tend to us. My grandfather was the strong, silent type. He would leave the house around 6 a.m daily to go to work. He made sure that the family was provided for as well.

Mom & Dad

I was very young when my mom and dad broke up. I used to ask my mother questions from time to time trying to get answers to why they weren't together. I remember her telling me things like "We don't want to be with each other anymore," "Your dad is crazy," or "I'll explain it to you when you get older." As time went on she started to give specific details of why they weren't together anymore. My mom told me that my dad had sex with one of our cousins while she was pregnant with me. She also told me that she forgave him for that. She said the main reason why she left him was due to the lifestyle he chose to live. She told me he went from having a lucrative, legit job to becoming a drug dealer. If you knew my mom you would know that is something she doesn't agree with. She used to say she couldn't understand how people could sell poison to their own people. She also told me that she didn't want me to grow up idolizing him or the lifestyle he lived, so she decided to end the relationship.

My dad's attitude was totally different. He understood how my mom felt back then but he told me he had to do what he had to do. He used to say that it was all about the money and if they didn't buy it from him they would buy it from someone else. He would say, "Why would I work a job when I can make more money in a couple of days than they would make in a month?" My dad had a bunch of stories about his drug dealing fiascoes that he would share with me throughout the years.

Due to his occupation, he ended up in different jails and penitentiaries throughout the United States. I can remember vividly my grandmother accepting phone calls so that I could talk to him. My mother would let me talk to him but she no longer had words for him anymore.

The next time I seen my dad I was seven years old. I was in the lobby of my building hanging out with my friends. I was throwing a ball up against the wall. The front door opened and a man walked in with kids. I didn't really pay attention to them at first; I just kept throwing the ball up against the wall. As he walked toward me I looked up. He asked me if I knew who he was. I said "Yes, you're my dad." He said "Yes, I am," laughed and gave me a hug. I looked at the two kids that were standing next to him. He said "This is your sister Deidra and your brother Little Sonny." My friend screamed out "That's your dad? You look just like him!" I was kind of in a daze. I was happy to see my dad but was confused at the same time. I was just introduced to a brother and sister that I didn't even know I had. We got on the elevator and went to the 11th floor which was the floor I lived on. We got off the elevator and my dad said "Let your sister knock on the door." Deidra preceded to knock on the door. My mother opened the door and said, "How can I help you?" Deidra pointed toward us. My mom looked and saw my dad and her expression and demeanor completely changed and it wasn't for the better.

I really had fun that day. I got to hang out and get to know my new brother and sister. I found out they were both older than me. Sonny was 12, and Deidra was 13. They got to meet my grandparents, mom, and little brother. My dad was catching up with my grandmother who he was always cool with. Deidra was complimenting my little brother Sean who was 2 years old at the time. She was saying how cute he was and was fascinated by his long hair. Sean used to get mistaken for a girl from time to time because his hair was so long. Deidra, Sonny and I went outside. I introduced them to some of my friends. Sonny and I played with them. One of my grandmother's Godsons saw Deidra and was smitten. They sat on the bench talking to each other. It was a good day until my dad announced that they were leaving. I wanted to go with them but was told I couldn't. Like the old saying goes "Good things do come to an end."

I wonder how my mother must've felt that day. She found out my dad was married when they were together and he also had kids that she knew nothing about. That day changed my life forever. It was like a gift and a curse at the same time.

Friends

I will never forget my friend Gary. He was one of my first best friends. He was a year older than me. We lived in the same building and went to the same Catholic school. We used to have a lot of fun together. His family was so nice to me. His mom decided to move the family out of the projects. She said that she wanted to move them to a better neighborhood. A little while after that they were living in a new place. Gary and I still saw each other at school and still spoke on the phone.

When we got out of school for the summer, I went to Philadelphia to visit my Aunt Estelle and Uncle Richard. I had fun hanging out with my older cousins. I wanted to fit in so I did some of the stuff they were doing. I smoked weed, drank beer and learned how to shoot dice. I was having a ball.

My vacation ended abruptly with one phone call. My aunt told me to come to the phone. I couldn't believe what I heard on the other line. My friend Gary was hit by an 18-wheeler while riding a bike and died instantly. I was standing there holding the phone crying. I was numb. My grandmother told me that my Uncle Reuben was coming from New York to get me. The next day I was on my way back to Brooklyn. I didn't want to go to the funeral. I wasn't ready for the tears, screams, sobs, or seeing the casket with my friend inside. I ended up going to the funeral to say my final goodbye to my friend and brother from another mother. They had to keep the casket closed because he had been decapitated. There were so many flowers, colorful and assorted near the casket. I remember people talking about how good a child he was. I cried my heart out as my feelings began to overwhelm me. I wasn't ready for my friend to go. I really believed he was in a better place. One of my real friends in life gone too soon.

My friend Jason was a real cool dude. He lived in the projects across the street from me. I used to go to his house to hang out and play video games. I had a lot of fun hanging out with him. He had two sisters; one was 12 and the other 13. The older sister used to say little things to me like "I can't wait until you get older" or "You're going to be my little boyfriend." I went over to Jason's house one day when his parents weren't home. We were in his room playing around. His two sisters, his cousin, and another girl from the building came in a room with us. His older sister started flirting with me as usual. This time things took a different route, the verbal became physical. She was laying on the bed looking up at me. She asked me to come sit next to her. She then asked me if I liked her and I said "Yeah." She said "Okay, you're my little boyfriend now." She then asked me "Can I see it?" I was scared. A nervous feeling came over me. I was caught off guard by what she was saying. The next thing I knew she was opening my pants. I was like "What are you doing?" She said, "Don't worry, I'm not going to hurt you." She then proceeded to put her mouth on it. I could tell this wasn't her first time. The sexual acts went on for an hour or so. I was nine years old and my virginity was completely taken from me. I could remember walking home from their house hearing Jason's sister voice telling me not to tell anyone and I didn't. My outlook toward females changed from that day on.

My friendship with Jason changed after that incident. We got into a fight one day at his house. He picked up a hot sauce bottle off the table and hit me in the face with it. Blood was everywhere. Glass from the broken bottle was in my eyes. The fight was broken up and his sister and a friend walked me home. I went to the hospital and was rushed to the emergency room. They flushed my eyes out and stitched up the gash I had over my left eye. The doctor told me "You're lucky, you could have gone blind." I saw Jason maybe once after that. Someone told me his family sent him to live with family members Down South. I never saw him again.

I never really talked to anybody about these incidents and how they made me feel. I was a child caught up with all these negative feelings pinned up inside. I felt trapped in my own little hell. I started to act out more and hang with people older than me. Soon I started to do what the older kids did. My mom and grandmother used to tell me to stop hanging out with the older kids but I didn't listen. I ended up on punishment from time to time for doing dumb stuff. I was trying to find something to help me escape. Beer, weed and cigarettes became new my best friends. It seemed like they were helping me cope but over time they were deflating my inspirations, dreams, and hopes.

Playing In the Streets (Poem)

Years began to fly by quickly. In the streets, I began to play. Their unwritten rules I began to obey. Gunplay, stick-ups, drug sells, oh well. I had to do what I had to do to survive in this ghetto hell. Years of playing street games almost led to my defeat. Experiences of others showed me this lifestyle wouldn't last. It's funny how God will reach out in your times of despair and give you a pass...

I remember this day vividly. It was a cold dreary day. There was a strange vibe in the air—like Mother Nature was trying to tell me something. I made my way to the block I hustled on. People were telling me to be careful. They said stick-up kids came through and robbed, beat and shot at people on the block. I was like "OK, whatever, it's probably someone I know." Even this dude I chased up the block with a baseball bat a week prior told me to watch myself. God was talking but I wasn't listening. About 15 minutes later an SUV with tinted windows turned the corner and began driving down the block toward me. When they got close to me three people jumped out on the passenger side, one of them I knew. As I was walking toward him one of the other guys tried to rush me. We started fighting. I was getting the best of him. He snatched the gun out of the other guy's hand. I heard a loud boom. The next thing I knew I was flipping in the air like a gymnast. I hit the ground in a lot of pain. I looked at my leg and it was about a foot shorter than my other leg. The thigh bone in my left leg was completely shattered from the gunshot wound. The gunman came and stood over me with the gun pointed to my head like he wanted me to beg for my life. I said, "If you're going to shoot then shoot." This lady I knew started screaming out the window. A cop was running up the block toward us. The gunman ran and jumped back in the SUV and they sped off. The cop began patting me down asking me "Where are the drugs?"

The ambulance came and rushed me to the hospital. It looked like a cow was slaughtered in the ambulance I was in. I was rushed into emergency surgery. A rod was inserted into my leg. I was in the hospital for almost a month. I was given morphine shots and pain pills the whole time I was there. They told me that I may never be able to walk again. I used to lay in the bed thinking how I was only in my early 20s and I may not ever walk again. I slowly began to slip into depression. God worked it out for me though. It took about 9 months for me to start to be able to walk without crutches or a cane. I was so thankful! It gave me the ability to get back to the streets I loved so much.

I ended up moving to Philadelphia a couple of years later with my girl at the time. What my Uncle Ronnie told me was true, "You take you with you wherever you go." I resorted back to what I knew best, selling and using drugs. Almost 3 years to the date of me being shot, I was hit by a car. The same leg was broken again but it was my tibia this time. I was rushed to the hospital. I had to get another rod inserted in my leg. I was put on strong pain medication again. I remember my pain pills running out one day and I started to get sick. I threw on some clothes and was on my way to go buy some drugs. I was out in the snow on crutches. It took me about an hour and a half to go around 8 blocks. It was so cold outside that day. Tears were coming out of my eyes and freezing on my face. I prayed to myself in my head. I said "God, if You get me through this I promise you I will change" and so the change began. A little while after that I checked myself into a detox. After leaving the detox I checked myself into an outpatient program. While there I learned about the symptoms of addiction, how drugs affect you mentally and physically as well as ways to modify my behavior. My counselor suggested I make a meeting and I've been doing so ever since. At the time of this writing, I have 19 years clean.

I've learned a lot about myself since I started making meetings. I've learned how to open up and fully express exactly how I'm feeling. I've learned how to better deal with my feelings and emotions. I realize now that I stay as sick as my secrets, so I tend not to have any. I was able to go back to school and get 2 college degrees. I completely turned my life around. No longer am I a menace running the streets. Today, I am a productive member of society. I have 3 kids I love dearly. They have never seen me use drugs but they do know some of my stories. I also have a beautiful wife who I married in 2016 that knows my story and still loves me for me.

The tears, heartaches, and pain from the past no longer have a strong hold on me. I can live today without regrets, resentments or fear. I will continue to move forward a day at a time and not let anything stop me from being the best person I can be.

About the Author

Divine Warren is a Writer, Poet, Motivational Speaker and Relationship Coach. He has an Associate's Degree in Liberal Arts from Community College of Philadelphia and a Bachelor's Degree in Business Administration from Temple University. He's a father of three kids that he loves dearly. He married his beautiful wife Ira Warren in 2016. He has appeared on podcast, online radio shows and videos discussing various topics. Divine recently started a radio show with his wife on Spiritual Connect Radio called Divine And Ira Warren "As 1". Their goal is to reach and help people who may be going through adversities in their relationships as well as life in general.

He also has a Blog called What Divine Thinks. The name of his blog says it all. He has a book of poems and short stories coming out in 2018. His vision for the future is to start an organization called Divine Minds. This organization will be an outlet to help Inspire and motivate children to overcome hardships and adversity they may have been through in their lives.

Feel free to stay connected with Divine Warren on Social Media at

www.Facebook.com/DivineWarren
www.Instgram.com/WhatDivineThinks

LOYALTY AND TRUST

By
Christina Burleson

Trust and loyalty are extremely important in loving relationships and form the crucial link that strengthens the emotional and loving bond between partners. If love is truly genuine, its depth keeps growing with each passing year. Loyalty, which literally means being devoted toward one's duties, obligations, and relationships, is an important ingredient in a relationship that includes a wide variety of commitments and faithfulness that one is obligated to demonstrate and fulfill to the ones they love most. For me, loyalty cannot be said to be a compulsion that is imposed by external factors because it has more to do with one's personal moral value system and the kind of decisions taken on different occasions. Our behaviors that originate as a result of our own personal value systems and moral judgments are choices that we take in keeping with our own free will.

On the day of my wedding, I thought I had ridden off into the sunset with the man of my dreams; he promised me the world and that we would live happily ever after, but unfortunately, that's not the way my fairy tale story ended.

The man that I held up on a high pedestal turned out to be untrustworthy, a manipulator, a monster who was not only disloyal to me but also to his family and friends as well. I have been asked why I stayed married to this man who consistently lied, who threatened to knock me "the fuck out," physically attacked me, who refused to help with any of my bills but yet was always going on shopping sprees after he told me that he didn't have any money. A man who talked about me behind my back, got with his clients, created horrible nicknames for me, was verbally abusive to our daughters and attacked them by pulling their hair ... The only answer that I can give was that I tried to work it out for the sake of our kids because I believe very strongly in the sanctuary of marriage and what it means to be committed and loyal to one person. The man that I knew before I got married was not the man I knew after we got married. He is what I like to call a Dr. Jekyll and Mr. Hyde.

When I met my ex-husband, I was only 24, a young naïve girl, an Airman serving in the Air Force, with the whole world at my fingertips. For the first six months of marriage, my ex-husband and I lived apart because I had to finish out my overseas tour in Germany. Once I had completed my tour, I moved to Las Vegas to be with him. It was a very exciting time for me because I had not seen my husband, and I, just like anyone else, was looking to start and building a life with my partner. Not long after I returned to the states, we started looking at houses, trying to find the perfect home for us and the baby that was growing inside of me. Life was good; I felt as if I was on top of the world. Everyone was excited for me and for the baby that I was going to have.

I guess the first time I got a sense of what his true personality was when we were looking at houses, and I had made a comment that maybe we shouldn't buy because we did not know how long we were going to be living in Las Vegas since we were both serving in the military. Out of nowhere, he starts screaming at me and pulling a tantrum like a five-year-old, stating how he didn't want to have to pay someone else's mortgage. So, as a spouse does, I went along with buying a house. After we moved into the house, everything was fine up until the point I had a miscarriage; it was a very sad day for me, and it took some time to get over the loss. The following year, exactly on the same date that I had my miscarriage from the year prior, I found out that I was pregnant with my oldest daughter. I had a mix of emotions because of the miscarriage I had previously. As time went on, so did the excitement of being pregnant. I was so excited about this pregnancy; it was one of the happiest experiences of my life, but as far as my ex-husband, his attitude would often change. He refused to go to any of the prenatal appointments that I had. He didn't want to go to the parenting class that I had signed up for because football was much more important to him.

Every time we were out with friends, he would put on his mask about how 'happy' he was, even though he was distant and cold, and all he did was hang out by his computer; he wouldn't even help with purchasing the crib and bedroom furniture. On the day that I went into labor, it was a normal day. I got up and was getting ready for work when, all of a sudden, this small pain in my lower back started. As I finished getting ready, the pain got more intense to where I didn't feel as if I could drive to work. So

I called my supervisor and let her know what was going on, so I ended up staying home. My ex-husband went off to work. I called the hospital to let them know that I had labor pains and that I would be coming in some time that day. As the day went by, the pain got worse, and it was all in my back.

I tried every remedy that my pregnancy books suggested to relieve some of the pain I was experiencing. I called my ex-husband up and begged him to come home. While yelling at me over the phone, he said, "I'm not fucking coming home unless we are going to the fucking hospital." I was so miserable, disgusted and horrified that I went to my bedroom and lay down and called his mom to let her know that I was in labor. I didn't tell her what her son said to me because there was no point. I was by myself, and I didn't have anyone to help me out. About an hour later, my ex-husband came home, and the only reason why he came home was that his mom called him and told him that I didn't sound too good over the phone. So I grabbed my bag that I had packed, and we went over to the hospital, and they did their checks to make sure everything was moving along smoothly.

Even though I was having contractions about every 5 minutes, I was only dilated at a three, and they weren't going to keep me at the hospital because I wasn't dilated at a four, and my water had not broken yet. While I was waiting for the doctors, the doctors informed me they had no choice but to keep me because the urine test they had me do indicated that I had preeclampsia, and they had to treat me and my daughter right away with medicine. So, they showed me to my room, and I got changed into my hospital gown. I opted to have an epidural, and they notified the doctor that was on call to administer the drug. While we waited, the doctor was able to give me another drug to help take the edge off the pain I was having with my contractions. So the doctor gave me the medicine, and right after that, my ex-husband told me that he needed to go home right away to take care of the dogs. When he said this to me, I shook my head and said OK, and he left. When he said this, I knew something wasn't right because I had been home all day, and the dogs had been taken care of. The man left me by myself at the hospital. I did not have anyone there for me to help through this labor. I honestly felt like a piece of crap.

A couple of hours later, while lying in bed, my water broke, and the nurses came in to change my sheets. They also checked to see if I was further along, and I was fully dilated I went from being dilated at a three to a 10 in only a few hours. Immediately, the nurse grabbed all of the technicians and staff and started preparing the room so I could push my daughter out into this world. My husband still was not back, and the nurses and doctor knew this, and they gave me two options: I could go ahead and have my daughter without him being there, or I could hold on as much as I could and call him on the phone to get him back to the hospital. I chose to wait for as long as my daughter allowed me to do, so I called him on the phone, telling him to hurry and get to the hospital because I was about to have the baby. He finally showed up, and after being at the hospital all by myself, I pushed my beautiful daughter out into the world. Once things had settled down, I asked him why it took him over two hours to take care of the dogs. I came to find out he really went home to shower and chill out in front of the TV while I had no one there for me.

The reason why I am telling this particular story is for one simple purpose: this was actually the foundation of how my ex-husband built his deceitfulness on. There was no loyalty or trust from him on the day which was supposed to be one of the greatest days of our lives. He really showed me his true colors when he was not there for me and how he lied about going home to take care of the dogs. Since the birth of our oldest daughter, over the years, I have had to endure so much when it came to him being loyal and trustworthy. I have had to witness him pulling many temper tantrums, especially when it came to him watching his own children. He couldn't stand it, but out in public, he made himself look like father of the year.

My ex-husband had two incomes coming in; he had a retirement check, plus he was running his own personal fitness training business inside the garage of our home. With both of these incomes, he made more money than I did but refused to help pay any of the bills except for half of the rent. He would always tell me, "I don't have any money," but every time he told me that, he was out spending money on $2,000 computers and TVs while I had to pay for all of the utilities, half of the rent, childcare, insurance on both cars, renters insurance, his football sports package, along with the cable and internet, and I was also expected to pay off a water system bill from the house we sold in Las Vegas. Thank goodness for my parents; they loaned him $3,500 to pay off his bill.

Not only was I struggling with all of his lies when it came to money, but I was also struggling with the disloyalty he had toward me. I would hear him training his clients downstairs, and next thing you know, he was just saying horrible things about me behind my back to people I have never met, and it didn't end there.

Honestly, I don't know how I did it, but I managed to pull through it. 10 years with this man, and I pretty much have been through it all. I have been physically attacked, verbally assaulted, along with our daughters, screaming at them and cursing at them. Always lying to me about anything and everything. I have had stuff thrown at me, holes punched in walls and doors, and him expecting me to work full time, pay off all of the bills and do all of the housework while he pretty much slept all day or was on one of his computers all night doing who knows what. He took some of my things that I had bought before we got married and sold them without me knowing. He also tried to steal all of my jewelry in the middle of the night; jewelry that I inherited after my grandmother died. And when I stood up for myself and the kids and started telling people what I had been going through, he would try to turn everything around on me, telling his family and friends that I was crazy and bipolar to discredit me. I lived in constant agony, even though I hid it very well. There was no trust or loyalty in our marriage because anything he told me was always questioned.

I wanted to share my story because I know there are people out there that are going through similar situations in their relationships. Living in this type of environment every day was a never-ending battle. With everything that happened, I was mostly disgusted by the lies and rumors he told about me to cover up what he had really done inside of our family. Last year was the last time I put up with him attacking me. The only regret I have is not calling the police that morning. The two beautiful gifts that came out of our marriage was our daughters, and all they are to him are tax write-offs. Even today, he doesn't take care of them like a parent should. Since my divorce, I still have to put up with his harassment and threats. For people going through this type of relationship, do not be afraid to get help. There are days that I still struggle because I have denied what had happened instead of acknowledging it. I strive every day to not let this abuse that I went through define who I am. Every day, I reminisce about what I could have done differently, and I don't think there was anything except getting help sooner for me and my daughters.

I am still angry and have feelings of hate toward him. I know that this will pass with time. Being a person who is religious and turns to God, I know I need to forgive him. How can I expect God to forgive me of my sins if I am unwilling to forgive people of theirs? When you forgive someone, it doesn't mean you become friends with them; it means that you leave that part of your life in the past and move on. If I could cut all communication off with him, I would, but unfortunately for me, I still have to remain in contact with him because of the kids. My kids are still reacting to how they were treated by their father. My kids were screamed at since they were babies, and even though they are older now, they still scream at me because they went through the screaming just like I did. It has gotten a bit better but not much, and I know they need time to heal as well.

If you have been in an abusive relationship, please do not

hesitate to get help. You need to take care of you and your family and surround yourself with a support group; there's plenty of people who have the resources to help you. There is hope take it from me. I am living proof. Never forget that loyalty and trust come in all forms, from words to actions; they are the foundation of any relationship. Without them, there is no relationship.

About the Author

 Christina Burleson is an Airman currently serving in the United States Air Force. She was born into the military life and has never lived in a place for more than four years. As an active duty Airman, Christina has traveled the world, holding various jobs in several different career fields. As a divorced single mother of two daughters, Christina is breaking her silence on the domestic violence she experienced while being married for over 10 years.

She wants to educate people about the warning signs of domestic abuse and how to escape from an abusive relationship while encouraging people not to be afraid to come forward. Christina, while still on active duty, is aspiring to be a leadership coach/consultant to help people find their passion and purpose in life.

Feel free to stay connected with Christina Burleson on Social Media at

www.Facebook.com/christinaburleson
www.Linkedin.com/in/christinaburleson

ABANDONMENT

By
Andrea Hamilton

My whole life changed one day out of the blue. I was in my fourth-grade class at Booker T. Washington Elementary school when I was called to the office. In the school's office, a Child Protective Services worker was waiting for me. My older sister and I were taken to our grandmother's home to retrieve our belongings, and the worker then drove us to a group home. I and my older sister were together but, we were separated from our baby sister because she was only a baby. She went to a real traditional foster home. I was really confused, but I made the best of it. At least I had a fresh start. In the home with my grandmother, it was not the best place for me to be; I was not favored at all. There, I received a lot of verbal abuse and some physical. As early as I can remember, I was reminded that I was a Hamilton. My last name stood out, and my features were of my father. My mother was in and out, but like every child, I loved my mother. I would cry and kick at the door for her to stay because I could not handle the abuse from my grandmother.

As early as I can remember, I wanted my father. I wanted

him to come and save me. I knew he couldn't be as bad as the family he left me with. He never came, but all I was left with was a picture to look at a picture of me, my mother, and father. The only peace and love that came out of the home was from my great grandmother I called her granny. She always told me I was pretty and played this little piggy with my fingers and toes. She stood up for me, but because of her age, she was unable to raise me when the State got involved. Everything I'd ever known was gone in a matter of seconds my whole family and my whole life. Even though the majority of my time I remembered from grandma's house was bad, that was my normal. We stayed at the group home for a couple of months until we were evaluated, and a home was found for me and my two sisters, and then we were all placed together.

I and my sisters met up at the home. My older sister and I were used to arguing and fighting because, at our grandmother's home, we were on different teams. She was grandma's favorite, and I was granny's favorite. My grandmother did not like me because she was not pleased with my father. I was only a child, so I could not understand this nor did I deserve this. I was just being a kid. My older sister did not last at this home because she was caught bullying me on several occasions. My mother was in rehab, getting help. She was expecting my brother; he was born prematurely and was brought to the home after staying at the rehab with my mom for a little while. This foster home was great. I began to open up and call my foster parents mom and dad. This was the first time that I had a normal life a real family with a mom and dad and sisters and brothers. This was the first time I could play happily and be a kid; the first time that I could go on a real vacation; the first time someone told me I was beautiful, and I actually believed them; the first time I actually had a memorable birthday; the first time that I did so well in school. It was rocky at first adjusting at school. I was the only African American. In my grade, I received the Most Improved Student Award. I had occasional visits with my mother; those were usually at Dairy Queen and lasted a couple of hours. I was always happy to see my mother, and of course, she was happy to see me.

She was getting better, but still, our family had a lot of work to do. There was a lot of abuse and some sexual that was basically never dealt with and swept under the rug, which turned into family secrets. These issues were addressed but not properly dealt with. My foster parents sat me down so that we could have a conversation, and I knew it would be about me returning home to my mother. If only I could have stayed in the moment. It had to come to an end one day my foster parents called me to the table to tell me that I was going home to my mother. I knew that this day would come, but could I live in the moment for a little while longer? I was last to return home because my mother got us back one by one. At first, she got my oldest sister back, then my baby brother and baby sister, and I was last. I was allowed to stay so that I could complete my fifth grade school year. Before I left, my foster parents had thrown me a party to say goodbye; they brought me summer clothes and clothes to put up for the next school year. Arriving home was emotional. My mom worked really hard, and I commend her for that, but she was a single parent of four children.

She started attending college while we went to school, and my brother went to daycare. She finished school and got her degree. She was trying to concentrate on school so that she could get a decent paying job and provide for us, but in many ways, we were on our own. My older sister was left to be in charge of taking care of us and the house. My baby brother suffered from asthma and bronchitis; he was in and out of the hospital. Times were hard, and things were stressful. I was not doing well in school. I began to get acne on my skin and also was diagnosed with another skin disorder. I did not have help doing my hair for school or nice clothes to wear, and I was constantly fighting, and especially with boys, I was angry. I and my older sister fought constantly. One day, we had a huge fight, and my mom called the police. At first, I was on my way to juvenile detention alone, but I was not going in alone. I had a knot on my head, and I told the police to take a closer look. We both were arrested and placed under house arrest. This was my first encounter with the juvenile justice system. On two occasions, I was arrested because of altercations with my mother; however, these allegations were false. Each time I went to the juvenile detention center, I was severely beaten. Lies were told that I had assaulted my mother.

The police was not on my side because, once you get in trouble, it follows you for the rest of your life even if you were the true victim. I eventually returned to the foster care system my 9th-grade year because my mother went back to using drugs. We were all removed except for my oldest sibling because, by then, she was a teen parent working and going to school. I went back to where I started. I went to the group home that I was at when I was much smaller. I did not do so well there. I was able to attend the high school where I was going before they removed us again. I would let the van drop me off at school, and then I would walk away from the school campus to skip classes and return before the van from the group home was there to pick me up. I would be intoxicated with alcohol and muscle relaxers whatever I could get my hands on. I was not drinking to try and fit in because I only had a few friends. One day, I skipped class and got drunk. I could not return to school because I had alcohol poison. I could have lost my life, but did I want to live anyway?

After this incident, I was sent away to a Residential Treatment Center in Henderson, Texas. This group home was far off in the boondocks; the purpose of going to this residential treatment center was to be away from my familiar environment and receive treatment. I don't recall a therapy session that helped me out. They were very short, and the solution was always medication. I never took any of the medicine that I was offered. I missed my family dearly. Did they miss me?

It was around the holiday season, and everyone was getting visits from their family. I was speaking with my mother when I could. She had finally gotten married. She promised to come drive up and see me for the holidays, but I waited and waited and watched as everyone had their time with their families. I was really sad. My friends and house parents tried to console me, but nothing could make me feel better. I no longer wanted to live without having a family. Why couldn't my life be normal? I went into the bathroom and drank some bathroom cleaner. I immediately passed out in the bathroom. I wished it was over for me.

I woke up to my house parent and the ambulance; everybody was freaking out. I wished that they would just let me be. I made it; I recovered but, I was still hurting. I then attempted to run away from school. Me and one of my friends were in the boondocks; we didn't get far. We had no phone; we had our backpacks with a few items in it. We stopped to use the phone at a house we walked past, and then the homeowner called the police on us. They were not far; we saw them coming, and we tried to run. They caught us. We were brought back to the home. While we were on our way, the police was handling us roughly. I ended up being wrongfully accused of assaulting a police officer. I was arrested. I was taken to a county jail in that county because there were no juvenile detention centers in that area. I stayed there for a couple of days and then was transported to the juvenile detention center where I was from. I stayed there for a couple of months and then returned to the group home where I originally started. Going around in circles from place to place. I was 16 years of age, with a 9th-grade education. I was behind in school because I moved from place to place.

I asked my Caseworker the state had given me if I could be placed in a charter school where I could catch up, or if I could be signed up to take my GED. I was told no because I was given a high level of care due to my history of running away. This gave me feelings of embarrassment, and my thoughts were, *I may as well run away because as soon as I turn 18, they will kick me out of the system with no education.* I thought and thought. I decided not to pack anything; I decided just to leave the first chance that I got. I listened to the staff and got up to level. They were so proud of me that I had come a long way. I was slowly getting privileges. I was with one of my favorite staff members. I had the opportunity to ride to Red Lobster. I held the door open for everybody to go inside, then I left. I hid out with family and friends.

A couple of months after I had run away, I met a guy, and he was much older than me. I was still 16. He did not mind because he had just gotten out of jail, and he had been in and out for most of his life. He brought me food and clothes at the time; all I could think about was what I needed. Child Protective Services came looking for me a couple of times, but they could never locate me. I partied and experimented with drugs and drank alcohol. My relationship was very abusive from the jump. I was never happy, only doing what I needed to do to survive. He was selling drugs and using drugs. 10 days before my 17th birthday, the state decided to emancipate me because I refused to return, and I had been gone for a long period of time. I got my first job. I ended up working there for a couple of months and quitting because my boyfriend would stalk me at work. He would get upset if I smiled and greeted customers. I was tired of fighting and wanted out of this relationship, but I had nowhere to go.

My mom came into town for a funeral, and I ended up getting in the car with her and leaving the city. I was 17 years old at that time. I had not been around my mother for a while and was hoping that things would work out, that they would be different. I ended up having a physical altercation with my mother, where again I was the accused. She ripped her shirt up and messed her hair up and told the police that I attacked her. These accusations were false, and even though I was arrested with a black eye, busted lip, and bloody face, the police did not listen to me because of my juvenile background. These incidents made me feel hopeless. When I got out of jail, I went back to the same place that I left from—to the same guy, to get the same abuse. There was nowhere else for me to go. I was so tired of this treatment that I attempted suicide again, taking a handful of someone's psych meds. As I tried to close my eyes and drift off to sleep, I cried to God. I said, "God, please take my life right now. If I can't get this guy out of my life, I don't want to live at all." I woke up vomiting all of the medicine. I did not tell anyone what I had done, but I woke up with a positive attitude. God must have kept me alive for a reason.

He landed in jail after this because he had gotten in some trouble. I felt happy and free; I could move on. I went on to start a relationship with a new guy, and I ended up getting pregnant. My first pregnancy ended in a miscarriage my grandmother passed away on Mother's Day 2009, and I then miscarried the following day; he was in and out. It was the worst feeling ever. This really hurt me; I wanted another child. I always wanted my own family so that I could have someone to love, and I could raise my children up better than I was brought up. In 2010, I had my first son it was hard, with no parents around for support. I had friends, and they had their families around when they gave birth. The whole birth experience was painful yet wonderful because I had my own son. 14 months later, I gave birth to a baby girl. I was not ready for another baby, but she was here; I couldn't do anything but love her and try my best to be a good mother. How do you parent when you never had parents or a real family life? I decided to leave my relationship with my oldest two children's father.

I then ran into a high school sweetheart. We had both had children by now, but he had gotten married. We began spending time with each other wherever I was, he was. The situation was very uncomfortable, but we discussed him getting a divorce. I was in too deep because he had always been my best friend a friendship I valued. I could talk to him about anything. He was everything I was missing. He constantly told me how beautiful and smart I was. I poured my heart out to him about the things that I had been through. We expressed our love for one another. I looked forward to seeing him every day. I'd gotten sick, and I was very scared. I knew I was pregnant, but I was embarrassed I did not want to tell anyone. I was already criticized for being a young single mother in the system. My biggest struggle raising my children was having a criminal history. The criminal history was family-related with my mom but it made me appear to be a horrible person, which I am not. I just wanted to be loved by the woman who birthed me, my mother.

While I was pregnant, I was very sad and depressed. I was broken from my childhood. I decided to place my son up for adoption, not because I did not love or want him but because I had no support, and his father was not supportive. I felt he was happy about this because this could be a secret. I read a lot of horror stories about adoptions and child trafficking and people buying babies, but this whole thing was new to me. I was making a permanent decision for a temporary problem. I was acting off emotions, telling myself I could not do it. I was already a single parent of two children who were 14 months apart. I chose to do an open adoption. I was promised to get visits and pictures. The adoptive mother called me every day.

Coming from a broken home and family, I did not have any support, which forced me to make decisions that would affect me and my family forever and leave me with Post Traumatic Stress Disorder, learning with age and time how I want my family life to be. Now that I am wiser, I've come to the conclusion that my mother had issues in her childhood, which in turn was pushed off to her children. She handled the situations poorly due to, again, not willing to address her own issues she was battling with. She pushed people away due to her not understanding or willing to appreciate genuine love. I, on the other hand, am working daily to not have my children experience a broken home and to learn from my trial and error.

After time had passed, the father of my son reached out to me to express he was broken after putting our son up for adoption. He expressed how he was not able to understand his emotions after the adoption, which caused him to disappear. I am taking one day at a time to not repeat a dysfunctional pattern that will not only affect me but also disrupt my children. I am determined to raise them better with love, support, and so much more.

Regardless of where you come from, we all have experienced some type of brokenness. We have to learn how to face the issues head-on in order for us to heal properly from the inside out.

About the Author

Andrea Hamilton is a currently a college student, a single parent of four children. She was born and raised in Texas and relocated to Pittsburgh to get a fresh start. Taking a leap of faith to rebuild herself and seek a peace of mind for her children, Andrea was able to find a new residence and employment fairly quick.

Even though it was challenging, she was willing to give it her all. She's determined to make a difference, and she knew it must start with her. Coming from a background of being a youth in the foster system can leave you psychologically damaged. Andrea is determined to educate others on how they, too, can break the cycle of remaining broken due to the system tactics.

Andrea is pursuing her Masters in Law and working in the judicial system to provide better opportunities to foster children.

Feel free to stay connected with Andrea Hamilton on Social Media at

www.Facebook.com/andreahamilton
www.Instgram.com/andreahamilton1336

A BLENDED MARRIAGE

By
Natasha Allen

In marriage, we find what we feel is the perfect husband or wife; once we get past the *I do* or *I will*, we soon discover that we all have things from past hurt, family hurt, and relationships.

Being married now for a little over 5 years, dating for 2 years, we both have our good days and our bad days. We both have menopause yeah, men, you get that too. Also, if you had a child or children before the marriage, it's really a blend that we have to adhere to, right? In marriage, it takes time for some, but there are 3 cords God, Husband/Wife, Child(ren). So, now that we know what our foundation is, we can build a marriage that will stand the test of time.

Communication

In the courting stage of relationships, we only see all that our mates want us to see. The communication is truly the structure of when we transition from courting to dating to marriage, establishing what our expectations are (e.g., standards of belief, whether he or she is family-oriented ...). We usually like our partner in the beginning, but when in love, we often lose sight that we liked each other. Having discussions during communication years is important, and this could include questions like: "What are your 5-year goals in life?" Keep in mind that simply because we say "I do" doesn't mean our reflections will always align.

Early in the relationship, we must establish the fact of knowing when not to push when certain occasions arise. Often we, as women, have to be vulnerable, as well as men, to let down the walls of past hurt from whatever we encountered. In our marriage, one is a full-time entrepreneur, and the other enjoys his 9–5 job.

Natasha grew up with two loving parents who had been married for 33 years until God called her mom home. Natasha is the eldest of 2 siblings and a cousister (cousin/ sister) that grew up in the house she comes a from a very loving family often referred to as the Huxtable Family:

"Although we grew up not being a product of what we lived around, our parents kept us busy in church and with various activities. Every weekend, we were away, camping, spending time with other family members in a not-so-drug-infested neighborhood. My dad grew up in a single-family home with just his mom; my mom, on the other hand, grew up with both parents. My grandmother was a minister.

Growing up with the foundation of values, as I grew older I strayed away, as most children, doing it my way, not the way my parents instilled in me. In doing so, I became damaged. I lost the way of wisdom mentally knowing right from wrong. My way led me to be with the wrong guys; the club was mine every Friday, Saturday, and man my mama didn't play about being in church on Sunday. I ran and ran further from the church, and doing me was just fine. I got tired of running, got back into the church to soon discover the church hurt me the more, and this felt real, and 3 years later, I went back to myself. It's the church folk, rather than true Christians, that will hurt you. Yes, there's a difference between going to church and walking the right walk. I had to learn the difference that a church is like a hospital where the sick go to get healed. "Wisdom will lead you the right way."

Reginald grew up with his mother and later had a stepfather. Reginald is the oldest of three boys and also the oldest of all his father's children. It was a complicated family, but we all loved each other. We grew up in the inner city and moved around a lot. Looking back, his mom grew up with both her parents, and his real dad only had his mom until later being adopted by a guy who worked for social service and liked him so much; this guy also adopted Reggie and his two brothers as his grandchildren. Reggie lived with his folks, who lived paycheck to paycheck and sometimes having their lights and phones turned off. Learning that both his mother and stepfather were on drugs was very upsetting. So, whenever he could, he would cut neighbors' grasses, wash cars, shovel snow and do other odd jobs to have money in his pocket. Reggie was a good student as far as grades, but his behavior only grew worse. Eventually, he would hook school, sell drugs, and steal cars. By doing these things, his mother was left with no choice but to allow him move to his biological dad. This worked but for a little time. Reggie went to a trade school in Harford County, where he played sports, and his trade teacher, vice principal, and coaches liked him. They all would say the same thing: "Reggie, you are good in school and sports, but your attitude and behavior sucks." Reggie eventually got put out of school and was forced into alternative education by a judge. That's where his life changed because a Sgt. became fond of him and became his mentor. Through all the mile runs, push-ups, mud runs, and all the extra PT, he learned self-discipline and how to function with people, also earning his diploma at the age of 17. Reggie came home from military school and took charge of his life, promising his grandmother he would not grow up to be like his father, mom, or stepfather. Well, to end this little story, he can say he kept his promise. He is now a Youth Minister at his church, a loving husband, and a devoted, loving father.

Becoming the Husband

Being a part of a blended family is what God called me to be. First, let me say up until Natasha, I never dated women with kids, so when I first saw Natasha, I saw her daughter as well. We started out as friends, but after a few months, everyone else saw it before us. They kept saying, "Y'all aren't fooling nobody. Y'all might as well move in together." Long story short, we did. I fell in love with my daughter; she stole my heart, which made it so easy to pursue a relationship with Natasha. We dated for almost 2 years before I asked her father for her hand in marriage. One thing I liked about the courting process is that we always talked to one another. And I think that is one of the most important things in any relationship. When I really sit back and think about it, I really don't consider us a blended family because we talk to one another every day, and we treat each other with respect and love. We gave our daughter the choice of what she wanted to call me—she calls me 'Pops.' This girl is my life-size shadow. She is the smile I need every day. So, basically, for a blended family to work, you have to have a few things:

First, you have to have God as the head of the relationship. Without Him, everything will fail. Second, you have to be able to communicate. If you don't talk to one another, how will you know what's going on? How will you fix a problem if you do not know what it is? Side note: If y'all have an argument, and y'all talk about it, you should let it go and forget about it. Don't bring it back up in later arguments. Finally, with that being said, never go to bed mad or upset. In marriages of all kinds, you will have some bad moments; so, when y'all are upset with each other, please make sure you talk about it before you close your eyes that night. Tomorrow is not guaranteed.

Becoming his Wife

In marriage, there are never two halves that make a whole, and when we blend, we have no defined steps—only the usual walking up and down. We are a family. Being a blended family has taught me patience, how to compromise, some more compassion, and to PUSH (Pray, Understanding, Strength, and Healing) when your partner needs it most. As husband and wife, we have to tune in to each other's heart. Brokenness creeps into our adulthood if that little girl or little boy never really dealt with dormant things, which were only buried somewhere in their heart. The other piece that made it easy for me to fall in love with Mr. Allen was, he knew the Lord.

Looking at my background and my growing up, I can say I have become a full-circle woman that loves Christ, not ashamed to display it. It's a beautiful thing when your friend invites you to church.

If your partner or spouse doesn't allow your light to shine, pray for them. Often we try to change the other person just because we're married. We still have our own DNAs (God, others, and ourselves). We have to meet them where they are and challenge them to grow. Remember, a relationship has several layers. What took you years to put together can be taken off by the three cords. What's your spouse's love language? Your love language can open so many doors in your relationship. Ladies and gentlemen, just know that your partner's way of showing love may be different from yours, depending on how you were both raised. So, communication is very important in sharing. You may speak English; they may speak Chinese. However, this is not the time you shut down and start displaying a strange attitude. Learn how to learn each other's love language.

So, ready? Set? Action! Every day is a roll call, a new journey in getting to know what the day will bring for some of us. Be that wife that stands with her husband, encouraging him as well as he encourages you. The key to this piece is praying for your friend/spouse whatever name you give them at times, and you will see this likeness between the both of you grow stronger. Oftentimes we forget what got us to where we are today. Let's go back to those 3 cords.

Marriage takes three: you, your spouse, and God. It was God who taught us to love. By making Him the center of your relationship, His love will bind you together as one throughout your marriage. Often we PUSH our spouse because we see the potential that's in their life, even when they don't see it for themselves.

Our Daughter

His Flower, my Sunshine. In the courting stage in 2010, we shared many things together; however, it took me 6 months or so before I would allow Reginald to meet our daughter. Being a single parent, I had a certain standard that I wanted for us both, so I had to be the judge of whom I allowed in her space. Being a single parent can be hard when it comes to dating. As a nurturer mother's instinct is to protect her cub. Many thought run through your head of trust, values when getting into a relationship. As time went on, I began to notice that he may just be my Boaz. I was introduced to my husband's mother, and she immediately became fond of my daughter. At first, I was not comfortable, as I thought, *You want my child to call you what your grandchildren called you? Pardon me; I don't want my child confused. I'm just friends with your son.*

Mama L as I, after marriage, began to call my mother-in-law truly saw something different and beyond "Just my son's friend." Reggie began to get really close, wanting to play an intricate part in knowing more about me and his flower well, in a good way. It felt a little scary in the beginning; I shared with Reggie about things I wanted for her as far as values and a solid foundation were concerned. We came to see that we shared a lot of the same things for her. I remember the first time he had to discipline his flower; he cried himself to sleep, feeling she wouldn't like him anymore. What his flower had done, I didn't feel it was my place to cut her butt. In a relationship, we as partner/parents have to set standards in this case, the standard was, he wasn't her friend but her parent.

Once we were married, as the wife, I felt something had changed in the aspect of Reginald's lack of good parenting growing up. He would allow his flower to get away with a lot of things because he didn't have certain things, which caused friction. My Sunshine needed structure, especially children with ADHD (Attention Deficit Hyperactivity Disorder). There must be consistency in her daily routine. In our marriage, we truly have balance, which is needed most when it comes to parenting. Reginald is very involved in his flower's schooling, doctor's visit, and their bond is remarkable. Getting your spouse to understand your views can still be a struggle from time to time. Being on one page is very important. We've always come to a mutual understanding most of the time. One of the keys is: never fuss in front of your child or children, and always keep the line of communication open.

About the Author

Natasha Allen is the founder of Nurture By Natasha. She was born and raised in Baltimore, Maryland. The first in her family to attend college, Natasha realized after working in the school system for 13 years that she had to make a change to advocate more for her daughter in school. Natasha began to dress and speak of what it was she wanted, which was more time and freedom using her gifts and talents. With the entrepreneur drive Natasha has, she was determined to keep pressing to move forward. Natasha knew that it was more than the world had to offer. Natasha put her faith into action, making her daughter her WHY to push to become a business owner to provide a legacy she can pass down.

She is dedicated to helping other women bring awareness to their inner serenity, as well as self-care to the body needs, knowing all too well that families are having high blood pressure, diabetes, and many are dying from cancer more now than ever. She knew there had to be a better way. Natasha needed to help educate others on the importance of self-care. "As women, we are nurturers, and too often we forget to put the mask on ourselves first before we bless someone else." Natasha understands what it takes to build, lead and coach others using the basic steps: Show, Share, Connect, Listen, Offer, Recruit, Follow Up, and Repeat!

Natasha is passionate about educating others on how to find their inner peace by 'Nurturing' from the inside out and putting the mask on you first, as well as making your well-being a priority.

Feel free to stay connected with Natasha Allen on Social Media at

www.Facebook.com/NatashaAllen
www.Instagram.com/NurtureByNatasha
www.Twitter.com/NurtureNatasha
www.LinkedIn.com/in/NatashaAllen
www.NurtureByNatasha.com

ACKNOWLEDGMENT

To all the authors, thank you! Thank you for your transparency and resilience in sharing your truth in your chapters.

Thank you for trusting me in this journey and believing the vision God has given me. I am forever grateful!

Much love,
Vanessa Canteberry

About the Complier

Vanessa Canteberry is the Founder and CEO of InspiredByVanessa. She was born and raised in Chicago, Illinois. She's determined to continue to break the cycle of poverty, negligent, and unnecessary hardship. Vanessa worked in Corporate America for 20 years as a Secretary. After being laid off in 2011, she knew something needed to change, knowing she was a single parent of three. Vanessa was not able to obtain employment, and the mere thought of being unable to support her son attending high school and two daughters attending college was unbearable.

For that reason, Vanessa challenged herself. She took a stand on faith and changed her mindset. She's on a mission to educating individuals on the importance of transformation of the W2 mindset in life and business. Now, she is a business owner, Speaker, Mindset Coach, co-host on Motivate Social Podcast, Best Selling Author, working from the comfort of her home. She is also committed to teaching individuals how they, too, can become a business owner and overcome obstacles in their life.

Your past does not determine your destiny; make what seems impossible possible. InspiredByVanessa stands on FAITH and refuses to allow FEAR to void VISIONS that need to be seen and heard on so many platforms. She teaches you that you are more than a W2.

Vanessa is the Best Selling Author of Shifting Your Mindset and Breaking the Cycle of Brokenness, Co-Author I Am More Than, Do I Not Matter and the Compiler for the anthology Cries of a Broken Man and Screams of a Broken Woman.

Feel free to stay connected with Vanessa Canteberry on Social Media at

www.Facebook.com/InspireVanessa
www.Instagram.com/InspiredByVanessa
www.Twitter.com/InspireVanessa
www.LinkedIn.com/in/VanessaCanteberry
www.InspiredByVanessa.com

www.ingramcontent.com/pod-product-compliance
Lightning Source LLC
Chambersburg PA
CBHW071141090426
42736CB00012B/2189